Bearing the Unbearable

Bearing the Unbearable

Stories of Moral Injury in Disaster Response

G. C. SMITH

RESOURCE *Publications* • Eugene, Oregon

BEARING THE UNBEARABLE
Stories of Moral Injury in Disaster Response

Resource Publications
An Imprint of Wipf and Stock Publishers
199 W. 8th Ave., Suite 3
Eugene, OR 97401

www.wipfandstock.com

PAPERBACK ISBN: 979-8-3852-8701-7
HARDCOVER ISBN: 979-8-3852-8702-4
EBOOK ISBN: 979-8-3852-8703-1

VERSION NUMBER 05/13/26

This book is a work of narrative nonfiction. Some names, identifying details, and circumstances have been changed to protect the privacy of individuals. Certain accounts are composites drawn from multiple experiences. Any resemblance to specific persons, living or deceased, is coincidental.

Contents

Acknowledgements

THIS WORK DID NOT come from a single place or a single moment. It formed over time, across many settings where people showed up to do what needed to be done, often without full clarity, often without full resolution. The pages that follow reflect that accumulation rather than any one event.

I am grateful to those who work in disaster response in all its forms. Many of you will recognize the patterns in these stories, not because they are exact accounts, but because they follow the same structures you have moved through. You have carried responsibility in conditions that do not always allow for clean outcomes, and you have continued to act within them.

To those who have shared their experiences with me—formally and informally—thank you. What was offered in conversation, in training, in debriefing, and in passing remarks has shaped how this work was written. Not everything that was heard is written here, but everything here has been informed by what was heard.

I am grateful for colleagues in disaster spiritual care and related fields who continue to hold space for this kind of work. The willingness to remain present, to listen, and to engage without forcing resolution has influenced the tone and direction of this book more than any single source.

To the organizations that support this work—often behind the scenes—thank you for sustaining the structures that make response possible. The systems are not perfect, but they endure, and through them the work continues.

To readers who come to this book from within the work, I offer recognition. To those who come from outside it, I offer a way of seeing that may not be familiar but is grounded in real conditions.

And finally, to those who have carried weight that did not resolve cleanly—whether named or unnamed—this book stands with that reality.

Introduction

When the Work Breaks the Soul

THERE ARE STORIES WE tell about disaster.

They are the ones people expect to hear. Stories of courage. Stories of endurance. Stories of neighbors helping neighbors, of strangers becoming something like family in the span of a day. We tell these stories because they are true, and because they are necessary. They give shape to chaos. They remind us that goodness persists even when the world fractures. They allow us to say something meaningful in the face of what otherwise feels unspeakable.

But there are other stories.

They are harder to tell. They do not resolve cleanly. They do not end with rescue or reunion or relief. They linger in the quiet after the work is done, in the spaces where language falters and memory refuses to settle. These are the stories that do not make it into reports or ceremonies. They are rarely told from podiums. They are carried, instead, in the bodies and minds of those who were there—those who made decisions they cannot forget, or who were unable to act in ways they cannot forgive.

This book is about those stories.

It is about disaster responders—professional and volunteer—who step into moments most people will never see. Firefighters moving toward flame when others are fleeing. Nurses working through the chaos of triage when there are more patients than hands. Chaplains sitting with the displaced and grieving while knowing that comfort cannot fix what has been lost. Volunteers showing up with willing hands, only to find themselves inside systems they do not understand, making choices they did not know they would have to make.

We often say that these individuals are trained for what they do. And they are. They are trained to assess risk, to follow protocol, to make decisions quickly under pressure. They are trained to manage trauma, to function in crisis, to keep moving when others cannot. Training prepares them for danger, for exhaustion, for the visible costs of the work.

What it does not prepare them for—what it cannot fully prepare anyone for—is the moment when the work collides with something deeper.

There are moments in disaster response when there is no good option, only options that carry different kinds of loss. Moments when a responder must decide who receives care and who must wait, knowing that waiting may mean dying. Moments when they are ordered to stand down when everything in them says to go. Moments when policy dictates an outcome that feels fundamentally wrong. Moments when they say words of reassurance they are not sure they believe, because there is nothing else to offer. Moments when they survive and someone else does not, and the difference between those outcomes does not feel justifiable, even if it is explainable.

These are not failures of skill. They are not lapses in training. They are not the result of weakness or lack of commitment.

They are moments of moral collision.

In recent years, there has been growing language for a particular kind of wound carried by those who serve in high-stakes environments. It is often called moral injury. The term first gained traction in military contexts, where soldiers described the lasting impact of actions taken, witnessed, or not prevented—actions that transgress deeply held moral beliefs. Over time, the concept has expanded, and it has become clear that moral injury is not confined to combat zones. It is present wherever human beings are placed in situations that force them into impossible choices, or into complicity with outcomes they cannot reconcile with who they understand themselves to be.

Disaster response is one of those places.

Moral injury is not the same as trauma, though the two often coexist. Trauma is frequently associated with fear, with threats to one's life or physical safety. It is the body and mind responding to danger. Moral injury, by contrast, is rooted in meaning. It is the distress that arises when one's actions—or inactions—violate one's moral or ethical code. It is not only about what happened, but about what it means that it happened, and what it means about me that I was part of it.

This distinction matters.

A responder may move through a terrifying event and, over time, process the fear associated with it. But the question of whether they did the right thing, or whether there was a right thing to do at all, can remain unresolved. It can return uninvited, in quiet moments or in the middle of the night. It can reshape how they see themselves, how they relate to others, how they understand their work, and, for some, how they understand God.

Moral injury often does not announce itself clearly. It does not always arrive with a name. It may appear first as irritability, withdrawal, or exhaustion that does not lift. It may look like a growing distance between the responder and the people they care about, or between the responder and the work that once gave them purpose. It may take the form of persistent guilt, even when others offer reassurance that nothing more could have been done. It may be expressed as anger—at systems, at leadership, at the public, at oneself. It may settle into a quiet conviction that something fundamental has been damaged, and that it cannot be repaired.

And because we do not talk about it well, it is often carried alone.

This book is an attempt to change that—not by offering a comprehensive theory, and not by prescribing a set of steps for healing, but by telling the truth as it is lived.

What follows are twelve stories. They are drawn from the kinds of experiences that responders across disciplines recognize, even when the details differ. Some are based on composite experiences, shaped to protect confidentiality while preserving emotional truth. All are grounded in the realities of disaster work. They are not meant to represent every responder, nor every possible form of moral injury. They are meant, instead, to open a window—to allow readers to step inside moments that are usually hidden, and to sit with what is there.

These stories are not tidy. They do not move neatly from problem to resolution. In some, there are gestures toward repair. In others, there is only the ongoing work of carrying. This is intentional. Moral injury is not something that can be resolved through a single insight or a decisive act. It is something that is lived with, wrestled with, and, at times, slowly integrated into a larger understanding of one's life.

If there is hope in these pages, it is not the hope of easy answers. It is the hope that comes from recognition.

For those who have done this work, you may find yourself in these stories—not in every detail, but in the shape of them. You may recognize the moment when something shifted, when the work became heavier in a way you did not expect. You may recognize the language of self-questioning, or the silence that followed an experience you could not easily explain. If that recognition comes, the invitation is not to relive what has already been endured, but to allow it to be named. There is a particular kind of relief, even if it is quiet, in discovering that what you carry has a name, and that others carry it too.

For those who have not been in these roles, these stories offer a different kind of invitation. It is easy, from a distance, to assume that responders are equipped for whatever they encounter—that training and professionalism create a kind of insulation. These stories ask you to see more clearly. They ask you to recognize the cost that is not visible, the decisions that are not straightforward, the humanity that persists in the midst of systems and structures that do not always make room for it. They ask for a deeper kind of respect—one that includes not only gratitude, but understanding.

It is also important to say what this book is not.

It is not an indictment of disaster response systems, though it does not ignore their limitations. It is not an argument against protocol or structure, which are necessary in crisis. It is not a call to abandon the work.

Rather, it is a call to see the people who do the work more fully.

To see them not only as capable and committed, but as human beings who are shaped by what they are asked to carry. To recognize that the cost of disaster response is not only measured in hours worked or resources deployed, but in the internal lives of those who stand in the gap between devastation and recovery.

The title of this book, Bearing the Unbearable, is not meant as an exaggeration. It reflects something responders themselves often struggle to articulate: that there are moments in this work that exceed what should reasonably be asked of any one person. And yet, in those moments, someone must act. Someone must decide. Someone must remain.

This book is about those people.

It is about what they face, what they carry, and what remains when the immediate urgency has passed and the deeper questions begin. It is about the space between what is done and what can be lived with. It is about the effort to stay human in conditions that strain that humanity to its limits.

If you read these stories slowly, you may notice something that does not appear all at once, but emerges across them. Not resolution, and not redemption in any simple sense, but a kind of persistence. A refusal, even when quiet and uncertain, to relinquish the part of oneself that knows the difference between right and wrong, even when that knowledge becomes a source of pain.

That refusal matters.

It is, in its own way, a form of integrity.

And it may be, even here, the beginning of something that can still be called hope.

The Moment That Ends

STORY 1

The Fireline Decision

THE WIND SHIFTED WITHOUT warning, pushing heat down the slope in a low, steady wave that pressed against the line like a living thing. Flames that had been holding along the ridge began to lean, then reach, their movement changing direction all at once. The air filled with ash, fine and constant, settling across helmets and sleeves before being brushed away without thought. A chain saw cut somewhere behind them, then stopped, the sound swallowed by the wind. The line held for the moment, but it no longer felt stable.

He stood just below the crest, boots set into soil that had already been turned once and would not hold much longer. The fire had been mapped, contained on paper with clean lines that followed the ridge and dropped toward the drainage on the far side. On the ground, the edge moved differently, slipping forward in places where it should have slowed, holding in places where it should have advanced. He watched the flame front shift again, the tips lifting and dropping as the wind pushed through. The pattern was no longer predictable.

"Wind's picking up," someone said from his left.

"I see it," he answered.

He kept his eyes on the ridge, tracking the movement across the slope where the brush thickened just before the drop. The fuel there had not been fully cleared, a section they had planned to come back to once the main line was secured. The fire found it now without hesitation, a thin run at first, then a wider push as the wind fed it. He adjusted his stance slightly, feeling the ground shift under his weight.

"Do we hold or pull back?" the same voice asked.

He did not answer right away.

Behind him, a crew member dragged a hose line into position, the coupling striking against a rock before settling. Another moved along the edge with a hand tool, scraping a shallow break that filled almost as quickly as it was cut. The work continued, but the rhythm had changed. Each movement carried more weight.

"Command wants status," the radio crackled.

He reached for it, pressing the button without taking his eyes off the ridge. "Line is holding but we've got increased wind and active spread on the east side," he said. "Requesting update on containment resources."

The response came quickly, but not with what he needed. "Resources are committed on the north sector. Hold if you can."

He lowered the radio.

The words settled without helping. Hold if you can did not change the wind or the slope or the way the fire had begun to move through the uncut section. It placed the decision back where it already was.

He looked down the line.

Six people, spaced across the ridge, each one working the section in front of them, each one glancing up more often now than before. Helmets tilted, tools paused just long enough to read the movement of the fire. No one stepped back. Not yet.

"East side's picking up," someone called from further down.

"I've got it," another answered.

He took a step forward, then stopped, measuring the distance between where he stood and the section that had started to run. The flames there were still low enough to approach, but the wind pushed them higher with each shift. A gust moved through, and the fire responded immediately, leaning hard into the slope.

"Get water on that," he said.

The hose line came forward, the nozzle opening in a short burst that darkened the ground for a moment before the heat pulled it back into steam. The water slowed the edge, but only briefly. The wind did not ease.

"Pressure's dropping," the crew member on the line said.

He looked back once, tracing the hose toward the pump unit further down the slope, out of sight but not out of mind. The system held, but only just.

Another gust came through.

This one carried more force, bending the flames low, then lifting them in a sudden sweep that jumped the break they had cut earlier. Fire moved past the line, not in a wide front, but in narrow fingers that caught quickly in the dry brush beyond.

"Spot over!" someone shouted.

"I see it," he said.

He stepped toward it, then stopped again.

The fire beyond the line was still small enough to catch, but the main front had not slowed. It continued to press forward, feeding into the same section that had already broken once. The ground between them narrowed.

"Do we go after that?" the voice to his left asked.

He did not answer.

He watched the spot fire take hold, the flames catching low, then lifting as the wind fed them. The line behind him was still intact in most places, but it no longer defined the fire. The fire had moved beyond it.

"Command, we've got spot over the line on the east side," he said into the radio.

The response came slower this time. "Copy. Can you contain?"

He looked at the crew.

They were already moving, one stepping toward the spot, another shifting position to support, the hose line adjusting again to reach further than it had been placed. The work continued because it always did. The decision had not been spoken.

He did not answer right away.

The wind shifted again.

The main front pushed harder into the ridge, flames rising higher now, no longer held low by the earlier cut. Heat moved across the line in a steady wave, forcing one of the crew to step back half a pace before leaning in again. The spot fire grew, no longer a single point, but two, then three, each one catching in the brush beyond.

"Can you contain?" the radio repeated.

He looked at the line again.

Six people.

One hose.

Wind increasing.

Fire on both sides now.

He pressed the button.

"We are at risk of losing the line," he said.

The words entered the air and did not come back.

Behind him, the crew continued to work, but the rhythm had changed again. Movements were shorter now, more deliberate, each one measured against the fire's advance. The line still existed, but it no longer held the same meaning.

"Do we hold?" the voice to his left asked again.

He did not answer.

Not yet.

The fire moved.

And the decision was still in front of him.

The fire moved faster than it had a minute earlier, the shift visible in the way the flames no longer rose and fell but stayed lifted, carried by the wind across the slope. The section that had held along the ridge began to give ground in small, uneven breaks, the edge slipping forward where the brush thickened. Heat pressed against the line in steady waves, forcing each of them to adjust their footing without stepping back. The air tasted dry, sharp, and constant. Nothing about it suggested slowing.

He stepped down the ridge a few feet to get a better angle on the spot fire that had taken hold beyond the break. From there he could see both edges—the main front pressing upward and the smaller fires spreading outward into brush that had not been cut. The distance between them was shrinking. The line no longer separated the two in the way it had before. It sat between them, thinner now.

"Spot's spreading," someone called.

"I've got it," another answered.

The hose line shifted again, the nozzle sweeping across the smaller fires in short bursts, knocking them down just enough to keep them from lifting fully. Steam rose and vanished as quickly as it formed. The water slowed the spread but did not stop it. Each time the stream pulled back, flame returned.

"Pressure's dropping again," the nozzle operator said.

He looked back once, tracing the line of the hose as it disappeared over the ridge toward the pump unit. The system was holding, but not at the level they needed. The delay between bursts had grown longer. The fire did not wait.

"Keep it moving," he said.

The nozzle opened again, shorter this time, the stream weaker but still enough to darken the ground. The spot fire dropped, then lifted again at the edges where the water did not reach. The wind pushed through, and the flames leaned hard, spreading laterally.

He turned back toward the main front.

It had advanced further than he expected, the edge now closer to the ridge line, feeding into the same section that had broken earlier. Flames moved through the brush in overlapping waves, no longer contained to a narrow front. The break they had cut still showed in places, but it no longer stopped the fire. It marked where they had been.

"East side's not holding," someone said.

"I know," he answered.

He moved along the line, stepping carefully where the ground had been turned and softened. Each position he passed showed the same pattern—work continuing, tools moving, eyes lifting more often to track the fire's movement. No one had stepped away. Not yet.

"Command's asking for update," the radio said.

He reached for it again, pressing the button. "We've got active fire on both sides of the line," he said. "Spotting beyond containment. Wind is increasing."

There was a pause before the response came.

"Can you reinforce?" the voice asked.

He looked at the crew again.

There was no additional crew.

No additional line.

Only the six of them stretched across a ridge that no longer held.

"Negative," he said. "No additional resources on site."

The radio went quiet for a moment, then returned. "Hold if you can. Additional units are tied up."

He lowered the radio again.

Hold if you can.

The words landed the same way they had before, offering no change to what he could see in front of him. The fire did not respond to them. The wind did not shift because of them.

A gust moved through, stronger than the last.

The flames lifted and drove forward, crossing another section of the break in a single sweep. Fire moved past the line in multiple points now, no longer isolated to the first spot. Each new ignition took hold quickly, fed by the same dry brush that had been left untouched earlier. The ground beyond the ridge began to carry flame in a wider pattern.

"Multiple spots!" someone shouted.

"I see them," he said.

He stepped toward one, then stopped.

The distance between the crew and the advancing fire had narrowed again. The heat had increased, pressing harder, forcing one of the crew to step back half a pace before moving forward again. The line behind them was no longer a safe position. It was simply where they were standing.

"Do we pull back?" the voice to his left asked.

He did not answer.

He looked down the slope beyond the ridge, tracing the terrain as it dropped into a shallow drainage. The ground there was uneven, brush thicker, the path of retreat less clear but still possible. He measured the distance, then looked back at the crew.

Six people.

One hose.

Fire on both sides.

Wind increasing.

Another gust came through.

This one carried embers further, small points of light lifting from the main front and landing beyond the existing spots. Two of them caught immediately, flames rising low and fast. The pattern repeated.

"Embers are crossing," someone said.

"I see it," he answered.

The fire had moved beyond the line.

Not just across it.

Beyond it.

"Command, fire has moved beyond containment," he said into the radio. "We are losing the ridge."

The response came quickly this time.

"Can you reestablish further down?"

He looked again at the slope below.

There was no clean place to reestablish.

No time to cut another break before the fire reached it.

"No," he said. "Negative. No viable reestablish point."

The radio paused.

"Copy," the voice said. "Advise."

He lowered the radio.

Advise.

The word placed the decision fully in his hands.

Behind him, the crew continued to work, but the rhythm had shifted again. Movements were shorter, more reactive, each one answering the fire rather than shaping it. The line no longer controlled the edge. It followed it.

"Do we hold?" the voice to his left asked again.

He looked at the fire.

He looked at the crew.

He looked at the ground behind them.

He did not answer.

Not yet.

The fire advanced.

And the decision remained in front of him.

The fire crossed the ridge in multiple places now, no longer a single break but a series of small advances that connected as they moved. What had been separate spots began to merge, flames joining along the slope and pushing outward into heavier brush. The line they had cut still showed in patches, a darker strip of soil against the lighter ground, but it no longer held the fire back. It marked where they had been, not where the fire stopped. Heat pressed harder against them with each shift of the wind.

He stepped along the ridge again, moving from one position to the next, checking each section without stopping for long. The crew adjusted as he passed, tools still moving, eyes tracking the fire more than the ground now. One of them kicked at a small flame that had crept close, then stamped it out and returned to the edge. Another paused long enough to look at him, then back at the fire. No one spoke.

"Pressure's almost gone," the nozzle operator said.

He turned toward the hose line.

The stream that came out now was thinner, breaking apart before it reached the base of the flames. The water still hit the ground, but it no longer carried enough force to push the fire back. Steam rose briefly, then disappeared. The line had become a delay, not a control.

"Keep it on the edge," he said.

The nozzle operator nodded, though the adjustment changed little. The fire moved around the water as much as it moved through it, finding openings where the stream did not reach. The wind carried it forward.

Behind them, a radio call came through, someone asking for an update from another sector. The response came quickly, too quickly to carry detail.

The operation continued beyond their position, but it did not reach them in a way that changed anything. The ridge held only what they brought to it.

He looked down the slope again.

The drainage below offered a path, uneven but clear enough if they moved before the fire reached it. The brush there was thicker, but the ground dipped, creating a natural break that might hold longer than the ridge. It was not safe. It was only safer.

"Command, we are fully compromised on the ridge," he said into the radio. "Requesting withdrawal confirmation."

The response did not come immediately.

He waited, the radio still in his hand, his eyes moving back to the fire.

Another gust pushed through.

This one carried heat with it, a sudden wave that forced two of the crew to step back at the same time before resetting their footing. Flames lifted higher, the sound changing from a steady burn to something sharper, more aggressive as the brush caught more fully. The ridge was no longer a working position. It was a point of exposure.

"Multiple fronts now!" someone shouted.

"I see them," he said.

The fire no longer had a single direction.

It moved across the slope and up it at the same time, feeding on what it found without slowing. The break line disappeared in places entirely, covered by flame. The ground beneath their feet no longer felt like a boundary.

"Command, confirm withdrawal," he said again.

The radio crackled.

"Stand by," the voice answered.

He lowered the radio slightly.

Stand by.

The words landed with no change to the fire, no change to the wind, no change to the ground beneath them. The decision did not move. It remained where it had been.

"Do we pull?" the voice to his left asked again.

He looked at the crew.

Six people.

One line.

Fire on both sides, now joining.

No reinforcement.

No reestablish point.

The wind shifted again, and with it came another wave of embers, carried further this time, landing beyond the spots that had already formed. Two caught immediately, a third flickered, then held. The pattern repeated.

"More spots!" someone called.

"I see them," he said.

He stepped toward one, then stopped.

The fire between them and the drainage below had begun to fill in, not fully, but enough that the path was narrowing. If they waited, it would close. If they moved now, it would still hold.

He looked at the ridge again.

There was nothing left there to hold.

"Command," he said into the radio, pressing the button again before the response could come. "We are initiating withdrawal."

There was a brief pause, then the radio answered.

"Copy withdrawal."

The confirmation came after the decision.

He lowered the radio.

"Pull back!" he shouted.

The words moved across the line, each crew member responding without hesitation now that the direction had been set. Tools were lifted, hose released, positions abandoned in a sequence that had been practiced but never taken lightly. Movement replaced resistance.

He turned toward the slope and stepped down, placing his feet carefully where the ground still held. The crew followed, spacing shifting from line to descent, each person watching the ground and the fire at the same time. The heat remained close, pressing at their backs as they moved.

Behind them, the ridge disappeared into flame.

The line they had cut no longer existed in any meaningful way.

The fire took it.

He did not look back again.

The decision had been made.

And it had already taken something with it.

They moved down the slope in a staggered line, no longer spaced for containment but for descent, each step placed with care as the ground shifted under their weight. The soil was looser here, less disturbed but less stable, small rocks rolling underfoot as they adjusted their footing. The drainage below came into clearer view, a shallow dip lined with heavier brush and scattered rock. It offered space, not safety. The fire followed.

"Keep moving," he said, not turning back.

The crew moved with him, tools carried close now, no longer in use but still held as if they might be needed again at any moment. The hose had been dropped near the ridge, left where it no longer served its purpose. The sound of the fire changed behind them, rising as it moved over the crest and into the slope they had just left. Heat pressed against their backs, not as sharply as before, but steady, present.

"Watch your footing," someone called.

A crew member slipped slightly, catching themselves on a rock before continuing down, the movement quick, contained. No one stopped. The descent continued, each step measured against the ground and the fire at the same time. The path narrowed briefly where brush thickened, then opened again as the terrain dipped.

He glanced to his right.

The fire had begun to follow the slope in uneven lines, not yet a full front but no longer isolated to the ridge. Flames moved through pockets of fuel, catching where they could, leaving small gaps where the ground held. The wind continued to carry embers forward, though fewer reached the drainage than had crossed the ridge. The distance between them and the fire held, but only because they kept moving.

"Command, we are off the ridge," he said into the radio.

"Copy," the voice answered. "Report when you reach safe position."

He lowered the radio without responding.

Safe position.

The words did not match anything in front of him.

The drainage offered space, but the brush there was thicker, the ground uneven, the possibility of containment unclear. It was not a place to stop. It was a place to move through.

"Keep heading down," he said.

The crew adjusted their direction slightly, angling toward a section where the brush thinned and the ground opened into a wider, rock-lined channel. The descent slowed there, not because of hesitation, but because the footing required it. Each person placed their steps carefully, avoiding loose stones that could shift under weight.

Behind them, the ridge was no longer visible.

Flame had overtaken it completely, the light now rising above the crest in a steady, uneven glow. The sound carried differently at this distance, less sharp, but broader, filling the space behind them.

"Fire's coming over," someone said.

He did not look back.

"I know," he said.

They reached the bottom of the drainage and paused only long enough to reorient, each person turning slightlyto assess the space around them. The brush here was thicker in patches, but broken by rock and open ground that interrupted the spread. The air felt different, cooler by a small degree, the wind less direct.

"Where do we set?" someone asked.

He looked across the channel.

There was no clear line.

No clean break.

Only sections that might hold longer than others, depending on how the fire moved.

"Keep moving through," he said.

The crew did not question it.

They crossed the drainage and began moving up the opposite side, slower now, the incline steeper, the ground firmer underfoot. The spacing between them widened slightly as each found a path that held. The movement remained steady.

A radio call came through, louder this time, the signal clearer away from the ridge. "Units on east sector, report status."

He raised the radio. "Crew is off the ridge, moving through drainage. Fire has overtaken primary line."

"Copy," the voice answered. "Proceed to secondary containment if possible."

He lowered the radio again.

Secondary containment.

He looked ahead.

There was no established secondary line in this section, only terrain that might serve if they could reach it before the fire did. The slope ahead offered some break in the fuel, a section where the brush thinned and rock showed through. It was not enough on its own.

"Keep moving to the rise," he said.

The crew adjusted again, angling toward the higher ground, each step taking them further from where the line had been. The fire followed the contour behind them, not as fast as before, but not slowing enough to change the distance between them.

"Water's gone," the nozzle operator said, lifting the empty line slightly before letting it fall again.

He nodded once.

There was nothing to answer.

They moved.

The slope steepened, forcing shorter steps, each one placed with more care. The ground held better here, the rock giving them footing where the soil had shifted earlier. The brush thinned in places, leaving open patches that broke the continuity of fuel.

They reached the rise and stopped, not because it was safe, but because it was the first place where they could stand without immediately needing to move again. Each of them turned, looking back across the drainage.

The fire had reached the bottom.

Flames moved through the brush they had just crossed, slower now, interrupted by the rock and the uneven ground, but still advancing. The ridge beyond was fully involved, a continuous line of flame that marked where they had been.

No one spoke.

He looked across the crew.

Six people.

All accounted for.

No injuries.

No equipment left that mattered.

The line behind them gone.

"Command, crew is clear of primary zone," he said into the radio. "No injuries."

"Copy," the voice answered. "Stand by for reassignment."

He lowered the radio.

The crew remained where they were, breathing steady, eyes still on the fire below. The work had shifted again, not back to control, not yet to anything else. It held in place.

He did not look at them for long.

He looked back at the ridge.

At the place where the line had been.

And at the fire that had taken it.

The decision had moved them off it.

But it had not left it behind.

They stood on the rise without speaking, the ground beneath them solid enough to hold but not offering anything more than that. The slope dropped away in front of them into the drainage they had just crossed, and beyond it the ridge burned in a continuous line. The fire moved through the brush in uneven waves, slowing where the rock broke it, then lifting again where fuel carried it forward. The wind had eased slightly at this elevation, but not enough to change the direction of the spread. The work they had been doing no longer existed in front of them.

No one set down their tools.

Each person held what they had carried off the ridge, not out of readiness, but because there had not yet been a moment to decide where those tools belonged now. A crew member adjusted their gloves, then stilled again, eyes on the slope. Another shifted their stance, turning slightly to see further down into the drainage. The group remained intact, but no longer arranged as a line.

"Command said stand by," someone said.

He nodded once, though the statement did not require confirmation.

The radio remained quiet after the last transmission, the channel carrying other voices now, other units reporting positions that did not intersect with theirs. The operation continued elsewhere, moving through the same structure that had directed them earlier. Here, the direction had paused.

He stepped forward a few feet, just enough to see more clearly into the drainage below.

The fire had spread through the lower brush, not with the same intensity as on the ridge, but steadily, filling the spaces between rock and root. The path they had taken down was still visible in places, marked by disturbed soil and broken stems, but it was already beginning to disappear under the movement of flame. The slope they had crossed no longer belonged to them.

"Fire's slowing in the drainage," someone said.

He watched it.

The flames dipped lower where the ground broke, then lifted again where the brush thickened. It was not a full stop. It was a change in pace. The fire had adjusted to the terrain the same way they had.

"Not stopping," he said.

The words settled without argument.

Behind them, the slope they had climbed held open ground in patches, rock interrupting the continuity of fuel. It was not a line, but it was more than the ridge had been by the time they left it. If the fire reached this point, it would move differently again. He traced that possibility without speaking it.

"Do we cut here?" the voice to his left asked.

He did not answer immediately.

He looked at the crew.

They stood where they had stopped, breathing steady now, the urgency of movement replaced by a stillness that carried its own weight. Their attention remained on the fire, but their bodies had begun to settle, shoulders lowering slightly, feet planted more firmly. They had moved through the decision. They were now inside what followed it.

He looked back at the slope.

Cut here.

The idea held for a moment.

The ground might allow it.

The brush might break enough to slow the fire.

But there was no water.

No reinforcement.

No time to establish a full line before the fire reached them.

"No," he said.

The answer came cleanly, without hesitation.

The crew did not respond.

The possibility closed as quickly as it had opened.

Another radio call came through, closer this time, the signal clearer at their position. "Units in east sector, prepare to shift to secondary containment on west slope," the voice said.

He raised the radio. "This crew is on east side, currently at upper rise beyond drainage," he said. "Primary line lost."

"Copy," the voice answered. "Hold position. Await direction."

He lowered the radio.

Hold position.

The words replaced stand by, but did not change what they were doing.

They remained where they were.

The fire continued below them, moving through the drainage, pushing toward the slope they now occupied. The distance held, but not because the fire had stopped. Because it had not yet reached them.

A crew member set their tool down finally, leaning it against a rock, then straightened again without stepping away. Another adjusted the strap on their helmet, tightening it with a short, practiced motion. The small movements returned, not as work, but as something to do with their hands.

He stepped back to the group.

"All here?" he said.

One by one, they nodded.

No one counted out loud.

No one needed to.

He looked at them for a moment longer, then turned back toward the slope.

The ridge burned behind the drainage, fully taken now, the line they had cut erased by flame. The place where they had stood earlier no longer existed in any form that could be returned to. It had become part of the fire.

"Command will move us," someone said.

"Yeah," he answered.

The response did not carry expectation.

It acknowledged what would happen next without reaching for it.

The fire reached the far side of the drainage and began to climb, slower now, working through the broken ground, lifting where it could, dropping where it had to. The pattern changed again, less forceful, but still moving.

He watched it.

The decision had been made on the ridge.

It had moved them off it.

It had kept the crew intact.

It had also left the line behind.

He felt that without naming it, the weight of it settling in the same place where the decision had formed. The two did not separate. They held together.

The radio crackled again.

"East sector crew, prepare to redeploy to west slope for containment support," the voice said.

He raised it. "Copy," he answered.

He lowered the radio and looked at the crew.

"Pack up," he said.

They moved again, tools lifted, positions shifting from stillness back into motion, each person turning toward the path that would take them along the rise and away from the drainage. The work resumed, not where it had been, but somewhere else.

He took one last look at the ridge.

Then turned away.
The fire continued.
The line was gone.
And the decision remained with him as they moved on.

STORY 2

Triage

THE AMBULANCE BAY WAS already full when the first stretcher came through, the doors propped open to keep the flow moving through a space that had no room left to give. Gurneys lined the wall at uneven angles, some occupied, others waiting, each one positioned just far enough apart to leave a narrow path down the center. The floor had been marked earlier with tape, but the lines were no longer followed, covered by wheels, boots, and shifting equipment. The air held a mix of antiseptic and dust, sharp enough to taste. Voices overlapped without forming a single conversation.

He stepped in behind the stretcher, one hand still on the rail as it locked into place with a short click near the intake table. The patient on it was conscious, eyes open, breathing fast, one arm held tight against the body where gauze had already soaked through. A responder at the head spoke quickly, listing injuries without looking down, the words delivered in a sequence that did not pause. A nurse leaned in, checked the bandage with two fingers, then reached for a strip of tape from the table beside her. She pressed it onto the patient's shoulder and stepped back.

"Yellow," she said.

The word did not carry emphasis, but it redirected movement immediately. Another responder took the stretcher and angled it away from the intake point, guiding it toward a section of the wall where others sat or lay waiting. The space closed behind it as soon as it moved. He stepped back half a pace to clear the path, then reset his stance without leaving the position. The table in front of him held rows of colored tape, already thinning.

"Next," the nurse said.

Another set of doors pushed open behind him, and a second stretcher came through faster than the first, the responders guiding it around a tight turn before bringing it forward. The patient on it did not move, head tilted slightly, breathing shallow and uneven, the blanket beneath dark with blood that had spread outward from the center. One wheel struck the edge of the table, shifted, then locked into place. The responder at the side spoke without waiting.

"Crush injury, lower torso. Unresponsive en route."

He stepped in closer, placing his hand lightly against the stretcher rail to steady it as it settled. He looked at the chest, then the neck, then reached for the pulse, adjusting his fingers until he found it. It was there, but faint, slipping under pressure and returning again just enough to hold. He lifted his hand and looked at the nurse.

"Red," she said.

She had already reached for the tape.

He took it, pressed it onto the patient's chest, the adhesive holding immediately even against the damp fabric. The color stood out clearly against the blanket. As soon as it was placed, hands moved in, repositioning the patient, clearing space, preparing for intervention. The stretcher shifted forward, pulled into the center where attention followed it.

"Next!" someone called from behind.

He stepped back again, the space in front of the table filling immediately with another patient, this one upright, supported under one arm, walking unevenly but able to stand. Blood ran from a cut along the scalp, slow now, the initial flow already past. The patient blinked against the light, focusing on the table, then on him.

"What's your name?" he asked.

The patient answered.

"Can you breathe okay?"

"Yes."

"Any chest pain?"

"No."

He looked at the wound again, then at the stance, the weight held unevenly but controlled. The patient did not sway. He reached for the green tape without looking down.

"Green," he said.

He pressed it onto the shoulder and guided the patient toward the wall, placing a hand briefly at the back to direct movement without stopping.

The patient moved where indicated, joining others already seated, already waiting. The space behind him filled again.

"Next," he said.

Another stretcher came forward.

This one carried a child, small enough that the blanket covered most of the body, the edges tucked too tightly along the sides. The face was visible, eyes closed, lips slightly parted, the breathing shallow but present. A responder at the head spoke quickly, voice steady but low.

"Pulled from debris. Unknown time down."

He stepped closer, lowering slightly so he could see the chest more clearly. He watched for the rise, waited, then saw it, faint, delayed. He reached for the pulse, adjusting his fingers along the neck until he found it. It held, but barely, the rhythm uneven, slipping and returning.

"Airway?" he asked.

"Unclear," the responder said. "No response."

He nodded once, then looked up.

The table held the colors.

Red.

Yellow.

Green.

Black.

Each one already in use.

Each one already placed somewhere in the room.

The nurse stood beside him, one hand already hovering over the tape, waiting for the word that would move the patient into the system that held everything else together.

"Tag?" she said.

He did not answer immediately.

Behind him, another stretcher pushed through the doors, faster than the others, the responders calling out before they reached the table.

"Severe burns! Airway at risk!"

He turned.

The patient on that stretcher was conscious but fading, the skin across the chest and neck burned, the edges tightening, the breathing rapid and strained. The sound carried across the room, sharp, uneven, each inhale pulling higher than the last. The responders guided the stretcher forward, clearing space before they reached it.

"Get them here!" someone called.

The space in front of the table shifted, one stretcher pulled aside just enough to open a narrow position. The nurse stepped forward, already reaching for equipment, not waiting for the placement to be finalized. The room tightened around that point.

He looked between the two.

The child.

The burn patient.

The space.

There was only one position opening.

One.

"Tag?" the nurse said again.

He looked at the burn patient, watching the effort it took to breathe, the way the chest rose and fell in uneven motion. He looked at the airway, already beginning to narrow, the burn pattern climbing higher along the neck. He did not need more time to see where it was going.

He turned back to the child.

The breathing remained shallow.

The pulse remained weak.

No response.

He looked at the table again.

At the colors.

At the order they imposed.

At what each one required.

He reached for the tape.

And the decision was in front of him.

He held the strip of tape between his fingers, the adhesive edge lifting slightly where it caught against the glove, then settling again as he adjusted his grip. The nurse stood beside him, her hand hovering over the table, already reaching toward the next set of supplies before he had answered. Behind him, another stretcher pushed through the doors, the wheels striking the threshold before rolling forward into the same narrow channel. A responder called out a name that did not carry across the room, then repeated it louder. The space did not open. It only shifted.

"Tag?" she said again.

He looked at the burn patient.

The breathing had worsened in the seconds since they had arrived at the table, each inhale pulling higher into the chest, the movement uneven and forced. The skin along the neck had tightened further, the burn pattern extending upward where it would begin to close the airway. A responder stepped in, reaching toward the jaw to adjust position, another already opening a kit without waiting for instruction. The sound of the patient's breathing cut through the rest of the room, sharper now, harder to ignore.

He turned back to the child.

The chest rose again, but only slightly, the movement delayed enough that he had to watch for it before it appeared. He shifted his stance, lowering just enough to see more clearly, then reached again for the pulse. It was weaker now, less distinct, slipping beneath his fingers before returning in an uneven rhythm. The child did not respond to the touch.

He looked at the nurse.

She was still waiting.

Not pressing.

Not looking away.

Holding the space long enough for him to move.

"Airway's going," someone said behind him.

He turned again toward the burn patient.

The breathing had changed again, catching now, each inhale shorter, the effort visible across the shoulders and upper chest. The responder at the head repositioned, lifting slightly, another reaching in with equipment already prepared. The stretcher had not fully stopped before the work began.

There was one position.

One.

He looked back at the child.

Nothing had changed.

No response.

No increase in breathing.

No improvement in pulse.

The blanket remained pulled up, the small rise of the chest barely visible beneath it.

He reached for the red tape.

His fingers closed around it.

He lifted it from the table.

Then stopped.

The strip remained in his hand, the color bright, immediate, the meaning fixed before it touched anything. Red meant immediate intervention. Red meant allocation of the limited resources already stretched across the room. Red meant movement toward the center where work was already underway.

He looked again at the burn patient.

The airway would close.

Soon.

He did not need more time to see it.

He turned back to the child.

The airway might already be compromised.

The pulse might not hold.

He did not need more time to see that either.

"Tag," the nurse said again.

He moved.

Not toward the child.

Toward the burn patient.

He stepped in beside the stretcher, placing the tape onto the chest where it would hold, pressing it flat with the heel of his hand so it would not lift as the work began. The adhesive caught against the damaged fabric and skin, the color standing out even as hands moved across it. The responders shifted immediately, the placement of the tape aligning with the movement already underway.

"Red," he said.

The word did not need to be repeated.

The nurse had already turned.

"Airway now," someone said.

The team moved without pause, one positioning, another preparing, a third clearing space. The stretcher shifted forward, pulled into the center where the work would hold. The sound of breathing changed again as intervention began, the rhythm altered by hands and equipment.

He stepped back.

The space closed.

The child remained where they had been placed.

Untagged.

Unmoved.

The blanket still covering most of the body.

The breathing still shallow.

He looked at the tape still in his hand.

There was another strip.

Black.

He had picked it up without marking the moment, the color now resting against his palm, separate from the others. The meaning did not shift with the motion.

Expectant.

No intervention.

No allocation of resources.

He stepped toward the child.

The noise of the room continued, but the intensity had shifted toward the burn patient, voices sharper there, movement tighter, equipment in use. Around the child, there was less motion, more space, the absence of urgency defining the area.

He lowered slightly, bringing himself level again.

He watched the chest.

Waited for the rise.

It came.

Barely.

He reached again for the pulse, adjusting his fingers until he felt it return, faint and uneven, slipping under pressure and returning just enough to remain. He held it there longer, not expecting it to strengthen, only to confirm what it was.

It did not change.

He looked at the airway again.

There was nothing visible to clear.

Nothing to reposition that would change the pattern.

Nothing to intervene with here.

Not with what remained.

"Tag?" the nurse said again, her voice carrying from the table as another patient was brought forward.

He did not answer immediately.

He kept his eyes on the child.

The breathing paused.

Then returned.

Shallow.

Irregular.

Still present.

He felt the strip of tape between his fingers.

Black.

He had not placed it.

Once placed, it would not be removed.

It would not be reconsidered.

It would define what happened next by stopping it.

Behind him, another patient was moved into position, the nurse's hand already reaching for the next color without looking. The room continued to fill, the flow uninterrupted.

"Tag," she said again.

He lifted his hand.

The strip of tape moved with it.

And the decision was no longer waiting.

It was in motion.

He held the strip of black tape just above the child's chest, his wrist steady but not locked, the adhesive edge lifted where it had caught against the glove. The blanket beneath it rose once, then settled again without fully dropping, the breath incomplete and delayed. He shifted his weight slightly, lowering one knee just enough to bring his line of sight closer to the chest without leaning forward too far. A stretcher wheel struck the intake table beside him, shifted, then locked with a sharp click. Someone called out a name from across the room, then repeated it louder when there was no answer.

"Tag," the nurse said.

He lowered his hand a fraction, not placing the tape, just adjusting the angle between his fingers. The child's chest rose again, slower this time, the movement faint enough that he tracked it by watching the edge of the blanket. He counted without speaking, eyes fixed, shoulders still, letting the rest of the room pass around him without turning. A responder brushed past behind him, their sleeve catching briefly against his arm before slipping free. The smell of antiseptic and heat remained constant.

He reached for the pulse again, pressing two fingers along the side of the neck, shifting position until he found it. It was weaker now, less defined, slipping beneath contact and returning in uneven intervals. He adjusted pressure slightly, then eased off, maintaining contact without forcing it. The child did not respond to the touch, the skin cool where it was exposed. He kept his fingers there longer than before.

Behind him, someone said, "Airway secured," followed by the sound of equipment being repositioned, plastic against metal, then a short suction burst. Another voice asked for a reading, and a monitor responded with a rhythm that had not been there seconds earlier. The movement around the burn patient tightened, then settled into a controlled sequence of hands and tools. The red tag remained visible between shifting arms.

He lifted his fingers from the pulse and looked at the airway again, the head angled slightly, the mouth partially open, no visible obstruction. The breathing pattern remained shallow, irregular, not improving with time or position. He adjusted the blanket once, pulling it down slightly to expose more of the chest, then stopped when the pattern did not change. The tape remained in his other hand, the edge lifting and settling with the small movement.

"Tag," the nurse said again, closer now.

He did not turn.

He watched the chest.

Waited.

The breath came again, shorter, followed by a longer pause that held just beyond what he expected before the next rise appeared. He shifted his stance, placing more weight onto his back foot to steady himself without stepping away. Another stretcher was guided past him, angled carefully to clear his position, then locked into place just beyond the table. The space closed immediately after.

He turned the tape once between his fingers, the adhesive catching against the glove, then releasing with a soft pull. The color remained fixed, visible even under the shifting light from overhead fixtures. He brought it closer to the blanket, holding it just above the surface where it would land. His other hand hovered over the chest again, ready to confirm the next breath.

Behind him, the nurse said, "Next is waiting," her voice directed toward another responder but carrying across the space. A patient stood just beyond the table, supported under one arm, shifting their weight unevenly, eyes moving between him and the nurse. The line compressed, the movement tightening.

He looked back once toward the burn patient.

The airway intervention had settled into rhythm, hands moving in coordination, equipment positioned and adjusted without pause. The patient's chest rose more evenly now, assisted, the sound of breathing altered but sustained. The red tag held its place among the movement, marking the priority that had already been acted upon.

He turned back to the child.

The breathing paused again.

Longer this time.

He waited.

Counted.

The next breath came, shallow, delayed, but present.

He placed the tape.

The strip pressed against the blanket just below the collar line, the adhesive catching immediately against the fabric. His hand remained there for a moment, smoothing the edge so it would not lift. The color settled into place, visible from where he stood without needing to be checked again.

"Black," he said.

The word moved into the room and disappeared into it, not repeated, not acknowledged, but absorbed into the structure that held everything else together. No one turned. No one stepped toward the space. The work continued.

He removed his hand and stood, shifting his weight back into the flow that had formed behind him. The nurse's hand moved past him, already reaching for the next strip of tape, already angled toward the next patient. A stretcher was guided forward, the wheels locking into place with a short, final sound. The space where he had been kneeling closed immediately.

"Next," she said.

He stepped forward.

The next patient was already there, supported under one arm, breathing hard but responsive, a wound along the forearm wrapped in gauze that had begun to darken. He reached for the shoulder, steadying them briefly as he asked the first question. The room continued to move around him, the rhythm uninterrupted.

He did not look back.

The space behind him remained where it was, unchanged.

The tag held.

And the work moved forward without it.

He stepped into the next position as soon as the space opened, his body moving forward before the previous gap had fully closed behind him. The patient in front of him was already being guided into place, supported under both arms, their weight shifting unevenly as they tried to stand on their own. Blood had soaked through the gauze around the forearm, spreading outward in a darker band that had begun to drip onto the floor. The patient's breathing was fast but steady, shoulders rising and falling in a rhythm that held. A responder at their side spoke quickly, then stepped away as soon as the patient was stable.

"What's your name?" he asked.

The patient answered, voice strained but clear enough to carry across the small space between them. He watched the face as the answer came, tracking the focus of the eyes, the way the head held upright without assistance. He placed a hand lightly against the shoulder to steady them, not holding, just guiding. The room pressed in around them, another stretcher already angling toward the intake point behind.

"Can you breathe okay?" he asked.

"Yes," the patient said.

"Any chest pain?"

"No."

He looked at the wound again, then at the way the patient shifted weight from one foot to the other, the stance controlled but not strong. He reached for the yellow tape without looking down, his hand finding it among the remaining strips. He pressed it onto the upper arm, smoothing it once so it would hold.

"Yellow," he said.

He guided the patient toward the section of the wall marked for delayed treatment, placing a hand briefly at the back to direct movement before releasing it. Another responder stepped in to take over, easing the patient into position among others already waiting. The space at the intake point filled again before he turned back.

"Next," the nurse said.

Another stretcher came forward, pushed quickly, the responders guiding it around the edge of the table before locking it into place. The patient on it was conscious but disoriented, eyes open but unfocused, breathing shallow and uneven. A responder spoke from the head of the stretcher, voice low but steady, delivering information in short phrases.

"Head injury, possible internal bleed. Declining en route."

He stepped in, placing his hand against the rail to steady it as it settled, then leaned slightly to see the chest more clearly. The breathing pattern was inconsistent, the rise uneven, the timing irregular. He reached for the pulse, adjusting his fingers until he found it, then held it there for a moment.

Weak.

Not absent.

Not stable.

He lifted his hand and looked at the nurse.

She had already reached for the tape.

"Red?" she said.

He looked again at the patient, then past them to the space beyond.

The central area was full.

Every red-tagged patient already occupied a position.

Each one already engaged in intervention.

He looked back at the patient.

The breathing had not worsened in the seconds he had watched.

The pulse had not dropped further.

Not yet.

He reached for the yellow tape instead.

"Yellow," he said.

He pressed it into place, the adhesive catching against the fabric, then stepped back as the stretcher was guided toward the wall. The responders moved it quickly, clearing space before the next arrival.

"Next," the nurse said again.

Another patient stepped forward, walking without assistance this time, one hand pressed against the side of the ribs. The movement was controlled but tight, the breathing shallow but even. He stepped in, repeating the same sequence, the questions moving quickly now, the answers shorter.

"Name?"

The patient answered.

"Breathing?"

"Yes."

"Chest pain?"

"A little."

He watched the movement of the chest, the way the hand pressed into the side, then released slightly before pressing again. He reached for the yellow tape, placed it, and guided the patient toward the same section as the others. The movement repeated, the pattern holding.

Behind him, the sound of the burn patient shifted again, a change in tone as the airway intervention stabilized further. A voice called out a reading, another confirmed it, the exchange quick and contained. The red-tagged cluster remained active, but no longer expanding.

He stepped back into position.

The next stretcher came forward before he had fully reset his stance, the responders pushing harder now, the pace increasing as more arrivals reached the intake point. The patient on this one was older, breathing shallow, the chest barely rising, the face pale against the blanket. A responder at the side spoke quickly.

"Pulmonary issues, oxygen low, declining."

He stepped in, reached for the pulse, then looked at the chest, tracking the rise and fall across several breaths. The pattern was weak but present, the timing uneven but not stopping. He glanced toward the center again.

No new space had opened.

No additional resources had arrived.

He looked back at the patient.

The condition was serious.

But not immediate.

Not in this room.

He reached for the yellow tape.

"Yellow," he said.

The nurse handed it to him without looking up, already turning toward the next patient as he pressed it into place. The stretcher was moved out of the intake area, guided toward the wall, the space behind it filling immediately.

"Next," she said again.

He stepped forward.

Another patient.

Another set of questions.

Another decision.

The rhythm tightened, the gaps between arrivals shrinking, the time between tags shortening as the flow increased. He moved through them, each one placed, each one directed, the structure holding under the pressure.

He did not look back.

The section behind him remained where it was, unchanged, outside the movement of the rest of the room.

The tag held.

And the line continued to move.

He stepped forward again as soon as the next space opened, his body moving into position before the previous patient had fully cleared the edge of the intake area. Another stretcher came through the doors at the same time, angled sharply to avoid the line of gurneys along the wall before being guided toward the table. The responders moved with it, one at the head, one at the side, speaking quickly as they pushed. The wheels struck the threshold, lifted, then dropped into place with a hard sound before rolling forward again. The room adjusted around the movement without stopping.

"What've we got?" he asked.

"Multiple fractures, possible internal," the responder said. "Stable en route."

He stepped in, placing his hand against the rail to steady the stretcher as it locked, then leaned slightly to see the chest and face more clearly. The patient's breathing was controlled, not even but not failing, the chest rising with effort but without interruption. He reached for the pulse, found it, and held it there long enough to confirm the rhythm. It held steady under his fingers.

He lifted his hand and looked at the nurse.

She had already moved toward the tape.

"Yellow," he said.

He pressed it onto the patient's shoulder, smoothing it once before stepping back as the stretcher was pulled away toward the wall. Another responder stepped in to guide it, clearing the intake space as quickly as it had filled. The movement behind him tightened again.

"Next," the nurse said.

A patient was already stepping forward, supported lightly at the elbow, the movement controlled but cautious. Blood marked the sleeve but had not spread further, the flow slowed, the wound contained. The patient's eyes tracked him as he approached, the focus steady despite the strain.

"Name?" he asked.

The patient answered.

"Breathing okay?"

"Yes."

"Chest pain?"

"No."

He watched the stance, the way the patient held their weight, then reached for the green tape. He pressed it into place and guided them toward the seated area, releasing his hand as another responder took over. The space closed again immediately.

Behind him, the sound of equipment shifted, a tray set down, a tool dropped and picked up again. The cluster around the burn patient remained active, but the pace there had slowed into a steady rhythm, the urgency replaced by sustained work. Voices moved in shorter exchanges, each one contained.

"Next," the nurse said again.

Another stretcher came forward, pushed harder now, the responders moving faster as the intake line compressed. The patient on it was conscious but fading, eyes half-open, breathing shallow, the chest rising unevenly. A responder spoke as they moved.

"Respiratory distress, declining."

He stepped in, hand on the rail, eyes on the chest, tracking the rise across several breaths. The pattern was irregular but present, the timing uneven but not stopping. He reached for the pulse, found it weak but consistent enough to hold. He looked toward the center again.

No new space had opened.

No additional red positions available.

The existing ones remained engaged.

He looked back at the patient.

The condition required attention.

But not before those already in place.

He reached for the yellow tape.

"Yellow," he said.

The nurse handed it to him without looking, already reaching for the next strip as he pressed it into place. The stretcher was guided away, pulled into the line along the wall, the space behind it filling again.

"Next."

The word came faster now.

The gap between patients had closed.

He stepped forward.

Another patient.

Another set of questions.

Another placement.

The rhythm tightened further, the time between decisions shortening, the movement continuous. He moved through them without pause, each one assigned, each one directed, the system holding under the pressure of the flow.

A responder leaned in close, speaking just loud enough to cut through the noise. "We've got more coming."

He nodded once without looking away from the patient in front of him.

"Keep them moving," he said.

The responder stepped back immediately, turning toward the doors as they opened again. Another stretcher came through, then another behind it, the line extending beyond what he could see from where he stood. The room compressed further, the space narrowing with each arrival.

He stepped forward again.

The next patient was already there.

He asked the questions.

Listened.

Watched.

Placed the tape.

Moved them on.

The sequence repeated, each step fitting into the next without break, the structure holding everything together even as the pressure increased.

Behind him, the section where the black tag had been placed remained still, untouched by the movement that filled the rest of the room. No one stepped into that space. No equipment was moved there. It held its position without drawing attention.

He did not turn.

The line continued.

The doors opened again.

Another stretcher came through.

He stepped forward.

And kept working.

STORY 3

The Pastor at the Shelter

THE FOLDING TABLES HAD been set in rows across the gym floor, each one covered with a thin layer of paperwork, bottled water, and supplies that had been opened and left within reach. Cots filled the space between them, arranged close enough that people could move through but not without turning sideways in places. The overhead lights stayed on, flattening the room into a steady brightness that did not change with the time of day. A low hum of voices carried across the space, never fully rising, never fully stopping. The doors at the far end opened and closed at intervals, each time letting in a brief shift of air before settling again.

He stood just inside the entrance, one hand still on the strap of the bag he had carried in, letting his eyes move across the room before stepping forward. A volunteer passed in front of him carrying a stack of blankets, adjusting them with one hand to keep them from slipping. Near the wall, a small group sat close together, speaking quietly, their heads turned inward. A child moved between cots, stopping once to look back before continuing toward a table where someone waited. The space held movement without direction.

"Pastor?" someone said from his left.

He turned.

A woman stood a few feet away, a clipboard held against her chest, a lanyard hanging loose at her neck. She stepped closer as he faced her, shifting the clipboard under her arm so she could extend a hand. He took it briefly, then released it as she turned slightly to gesture toward the center of the room.

"We've got about eighty here right now," she said. "More expected tonight."

He nodded once, adjusting the strap on his shoulder before letting it fall back into place. His eyes followed her gesture across the rows of cots, the spacing between them narrowing toward the far wall. A volunteer knelt beside one of the cots, speaking to someone lying down, their voice low but steady. Theperson on the cot did not move.

"Food's set up along the back," she said. "Medical's over there."

She pointed again, marking the sections without stepping toward them. The room had already been divided, each part holding its own function, its own movement.

"Where do you want me?" he asked.

She paused for a moment, shifting her weight slightly, the clipboard pressing more firmly against her side. "Just move through," she said. "Talk to people. Sit with them if they want."

He nodded.

No further instruction came.

A stretcher passed behind them, guided carefully between the rows, the responders moving slowly to avoid catching the wheels on the edges of the cots. The person on it lay still, a blanket pulled up to the shoulders, the face turned away. A nurse walked alongside, one hand resting lightly near the rail as they moved.

He stepped forward.

The floor gave slightly underfoot where mats had been placed to cover the hardwood, the surface uneven where they overlapped. He moved between two rows of cots, turning sideways briefly to let someone pass, then continuing on. A man sat at the edge of one cot, elbows resting on his knees, hands clasped together, looking down at the floor. Another person lay back with one arm across their eyes, the other hand resting at their side, fingers curled loosely.

He slowed as he moved, not stopping yet, letting his presence settle into the space before attaching it to any one person. A volunteer passed him carrying a plastic bin, the contents shifting with each step, the sound soft but constant. At the far end of the row, a woman adjusted a blanket over someone's shoulders, pulling it higher, then smoothing it once before stepping away.

He set his bag down near the leg of an empty cot, placing it where it would not block the path. The zipper caught briefly as he closed it, then released with a short pull. He straightened, looking again across the row, then turned slightly toward the center of the room.

A man looked up as he approached, his eyes tracking him for a moment before dropping again to his hands. He stopped a few feet away, not stepping closer without being acknowledged. The man did not speak. He did not move.

He waited.

Across the aisle, someone began to cry, the sound low at first, then rising slightly before settling again. A volunteer moved toward them, kneeling beside the cot, one hand placed lightly on the edge without touching the person. The crying did not stop, but it did not spread beyond that space.

He shifted his weight once, then stepped closer to the man.

"Is this seat taken?" he asked, gesturing toward the empty space on the cot.

The man looked up briefly, then shook his head once without speaking.

He sat.

The cot shifted under the added weight, the metal frame giving a slight sound before settling. He placed his hands on his knees, mirroring the posture of the man beside him without matching it exactly. The space between them remained.

The man's hands stayed clasped.

His gaze remained down.

He did not speak.

He did not move.

The room continued around them, the low hum of voices, the movement between rows, the doors opening and closing at intervals. A cart rolled past at the far end, the wheels turning steadily, then stopping as someone repositioned it. The overhead lights remained unchanged.

He did not begin with a question.

He did not reach for anything in his bag.

He sat.

And waited for the space to shift.

He sat without speaking, his hands resting on his knees, his posture steady but not fixed, leaving enough space between himself and the man beside him that neither had to adjust. The cot shifted slightly as the man moved his weight, then settled again with a faint metallic sound. Across the aisle, a volunteer stood and stepped back from the person who had been crying, giving them space without leaving entirely. The low hum of voices continued, rising and falling without breaking. The doors at the far end opened again, letting in a brief draft that moved across the floor before fading.

The man beside him drew in a breath that caught slightly before evening out, his hands tightening together for a moment, then loosening without separating. He did not look up. His shoulders remained forward, his elbows still braced against his legs. The posture held.

"You been here long?" he asked.

The man did not answer right away.

A cart rolled past at the end of the row, plastic bins stacked unevenly, one shifting slightly before being steadied by the volunteer pushing it. Someone called out for more water, the request repeated once before being answered. The movement passed through without settling.

"Since this morning," the man said finally.

His voice was low, roughened, not from strain alone but from use, as if he had already spoken more than he intended earlier in the day. He did not lift his head as he answered. His hands remained clasped.

He nodded once, though the man did not look.

"Came in with others?" he asked.

The man's shoulders shifted slightly, then stilled again. He drew in another breath, slower this time, holding it for a moment before letting it go. The pause extended just long enough to be noticed.

"No," he said.

The word landed and stayed.

A volunteer moved between the rows, stopping briefly at each cot to check something written on a sheet clipped to the frame before moving on. A child crossed behind them, stepping carefully between the cots, carrying a blanket that trailed slightly at one corner. The fabric brushed the floor, then lifted again as the child adjusted their grip.

He kept his gaze forward, not turning fully toward the man, letting the conversation remain where it was without pressing it further.

"You get out on your own?" he asked.

The man's hands tightened again, the fingers pressing together more firmly before easing. He nodded once, a small movement, then stopped.

"Yeah."

The answer came without elaboration.

The space held again, not empty, but not filled with anything new. The man's breathing steadied, the rise and fall of his shoulders becoming more regular. He shifted his feet slightly, repositioning them on the mat beneath the cot, then returned his hands to the same clasped position.

Across the aisle, the person who had been crying had gone quiet, their face turned toward the wall, one hand pulled up under the blanket. The volunteer remained nearby, standing now, watching without stepping in again. A responder passed behind them, speaking briefly into a radio, then lowering it as they moved on.

He adjusted his position slightly, leaning back just enough to change the angle of his weight on the cot, then settled again. The metal frame gave another small sound before holding.

"You got anyone here with you now?" he asked.

The man shook his head once.

"No."

He did not add anything to it.

A pause followed, longer this time, not waiting for a response, just holding the space as it was. The room continued to move around them, the same pattern repeating—voices, footsteps, carts, the opening and closing of the doors. The light remained constant, flattening the edges of the space.

The man's hands loosened slightly, the fingers separating just enough to shift position before coming back together. He drew in another breath, then let it out more slowly than before.

"They said we can't go back," he said.

The words came without direction, not aimed at him specifically, but placed into the space between them. The man's head remained down, his gaze still on the floor.

He nodded once.

"Not yet," he said.

The man's shoulders lifted slightly, then dropped again, the movement small but visible. He rubbed his thumb along the side of his hand, a repeated motion that did not stop once it started.

"My place is still there," the man said.

He did not respond immediately.

A stretcher passed at the far end of the row, the responders moving slower this time, navigating around a cluster of cots where the spacing had narrowed. The wheels rolled unevenly over the mats, then steadied as they reached a clearer section. A nurse walked beside it, one hand near the rail, the other holding a clipboard.

"They said it's still standing," the man added.

He kept his gaze forward.

"That's good," he said.

The man shook his head, a small movement that did not lift his face.

"Don't know what that means," he said.

His hands tightened again, then loosened, the motion repeating once before stopping. He shifted his weight slightly, the cot creaking under the movement, then settling again.

He did not answer right away.

He let the statement remain as it was, without adjusting it, without turning it into something else. The room continued around them, unchanged by the exchange.

A volunteer approached the end of the row, stopping to check the clipboard attached to one of the cots before moving on. Another followed behind, carrying a stack of towels, setting them down on a table before turning back toward the entrance.

He rested his hands where they were, not reaching for the man, not moving closer.

"You got anything with you?" he asked.

The man shook his head again.

"No."

The answer came quickly this time.

He nodded once.

The space between them remained.

The man's breathing steadied further, the rise and fall of his shoulders more even now, though his hands did not fully relax. He kept his gaze down, not looking up, not looking around.

He did not fill the silence.

He did not move to change it.

He sat.

And let the weight of what had been said stay where it was.

He remained seated beside the man, his hands still resting on his knees, his posture unchanged as the movement of the room continued around them. A volunteer passed through the aisle carrying a stack of plastic-wrapped blankets, shifting them against their hip to keep them from sliding. The fabric brushed lightly against the edge of the cot as they moved past, then cleared. The man beside him did not look up.

At the far end of the row, a responder stopped beside a cot and leaned in to speak, their voice low and steady, then straightened and moved on without waiting for a response. The cart that had passed earlier returned, the bins rearranged, one lid left slightly open so the contents inside shifted with each step. Someone called out for a name near the entrance, then repeated it louder when no one answered. The sound carried across the gym and settled without resolution.

The man beside him drew in another breath, slower this time, then let it out through his nose, the movement controlled but not relaxed. His hands shifted again, fingers separating briefly before pressing back together, the motion small and repeated. He leaned forward slightly, then stopped, his elbows still resting on his knees. The posture held.

"They got a list," the man said.

He did not turn toward him, keeping his gaze forward, letting the words remain where they were placed. A volunteer crossed the aisle ahead of them, stopping at a cot to adjust a pillow before moving on. The overhead lights hummed without change.

"Names," the man added.

He nodded once.

"They're working through it," he said.

The man's shoulders lifted slightly, then dropped again, the motion uneven. He rubbed his thumb along the side of his hand, the same motion as before, then stopped it midway through and let his hand rest again.

"She's not on it," the man said.

The words came lower this time, closer to the floor than to him, not directed but not withheld.

He kept his posture the same, his hands still where they had been.

"Who?" he asked.

The man did not answer immediately.

A child moved past at the end of the row, stepping carefully between the cots, one hand holding onto the edge of a blanket wrapped around their shoulders. They paused once, looking toward the entrance, then continued on. The doors opened again, letting in a brief current of cooler air before closing.

"My wife," the man said.

He nodded once.

"Okay," he said.

The man's hands tightened again, the fingers pressing into each other more firmly, then loosening just enough to shift position. He leaned forward a little more this time, his shoulders rounding further, his head dropping slightly.

"They got her name wrong the first time," he said. "Spelled it wrong."

He listened without interrupting.

"They said they'd fix it," the man continued. "Said it'd show up next time they printed it."

The man's voice held steady, but the words came slower now, spaced further apart. He drew in another breath, held it briefly, then let it out.

"It didn't."

The statement settled.

Across the aisle, someone stood from a cot and took a few steps toward the tables, then stopped as a volunteer met them halfway, guiding them gently back. The movement was quiet, controlled, already finished before it drew attention.

He shifted his weight slightly, leaning back just enough to ease the pressure on the cot, then settled again. The metal frame gave a small sound, then held.

"They're still updating," he said.

The man shook his head once.

"They keep saying that," he said.

His hands moved again, one hand lifting slightly before settling back down, the fingers no longer fully clasped but not separated either. He looked down at the floor, his gaze fixed on a spot just ahead of his feet.

"They told me to wait," he said.

He nodded.

"That's what they'll say," he replied.

The man's shoulders lifted again, then dropped, the movement sharper this time before settling. He rubbed his hands together once, then stopped, placing them back on his knees in the same position as before.

"I went back to the street," the man said.

He did not move.

"They had it blocked," the man continued. "Tape across the whole thing."

He could see it without asking.

"National Guard," the man said.

The word came out flat, without emphasis.

"They wouldn't let anyone through."

A responder passed behind them, speaking briefly into a radio, then lowering it as they moved toward the entrance. The doors opened again, the sound of vehicles outside carrying in for a moment before the doors closed and the noise settled back into the room.

"I told them my house was still there," the man said. "Told them I just needed to check."

He nodded once.

"They didn't move," the man added.

The man's hands tightened again, then loosened, the motion slower now, less repeated. He leaned back slightly, shifting his weight on the cot, then settled again.

"They just stood there," he said.

The statement remained.

He did not answer right away.

He let the words sit where they were, not adjusting them, not adding to them. The room continued to move around them, the same pattern of voices, footsteps, and quiet exchanges holding steady.

A volunteer approached the end of the row, stopping to check a clipboard attached to one of the cots before moving on. Another followed behind, carrying a box of supplies, setting it down on a table before turning back toward the entrance.

He kept his hands on his knees.

He did not reach out.

He did not shift closer.

"You hear anything else about her?" he asked.

The man shook his head.

"No."

The answer came quickly, without pause.

The space between them held again.

The man's breathing remained steady, though his hands did not fully relax. He kept his gaze down, fixed in the same place, not lifting it.

He did not fill the silence.

He did not move to change it.

He stayed.

And let the words that had been spoken remain where they were.

He remained seated beside the man, his hands still resting on his knees, his posture unchanged as the room continued to move around them. A volunteer pushed a cart down the aisle, the wheels catching briefly on the edge of a mat before rolling free, the bins on top shifting with a dull plastic sound. Someone near the entrance called out another name, the voice raised enough to carry across the gym, then lowered again when there was no response. The overhead lights held steady, flattening the space without shadow. The man beside him did not look up.

The man drew in a breath, deeper this time, then let it out slowly, the movement more controlled than before but still uneven at the end. His hands shifted again, one hand lifting slightly before settling back down, the fingers no longer pressed tightly together. He leaned back a fraction, just enough to change the pressure on his elbows, then returned to the same forward posture. The cot creaked softly under the adjustment. The space between them remained unchanged.

"They had a list out front too," the man said.

He kept his gaze forward, letting the words sit where they were placed. A responder moved past behind them, speaking briefly into a radio, then lowering it as they reached the far end of the row. A child laughed somewhere near the tables, the sound brief and out of place, then gone.

"Different list," the man added.

He nodded once.

"From the street," the man said. "Names of houses."

He listened without interrupting.

"They marked them," the man continued. "Standing. Gone. Unsafe."

The man's voice held steady, but the spacing between the words widened, each one placed more deliberately than the last. He rubbed his thumb along the side of his hand again, then stopped halfway through the motion.

"My place was on it," he said.

He did not respond immediately.

A volunteer stepped into the aisle ahead of them, pausing to adjust a blanket that had slipped from a cot, then smoothing it once before moving on. The movement was quiet, already finished before it drew attention.

"What did it say?" he asked.

The man did not answer right away.

He shifted his weight again, leaning forward slightly, his elbows pressing more firmly into his knees. His hands tightened once, then loosened, the motion slower now, less repeated.

"Standing," he said.

The word landed without emphasis.

He nodded once.

"That's something," he said.

The man shook his head again, a small movement that did not lift his face.

"She's not there," he said.

The statement remained between them.

Across the aisle, someone sat up from a cot and swung their legs over the side, pausing before standing as a volunteer stepped in to steady them. The movement was controlled, guided, then complete. The space closed again.

"They wouldn't let me go back," the man said.

He kept his posture the same, his hands still resting where they had been.

"They said it's not safe," the man continued. "Said I had to wait."

The man's shoulders lifted slightly, then dropped again, the motion uneven. He pressed his hands together once more, then let them rest again.

"I told them I just needed five minutes," he said.

He nodded once.

"They didn't move," the man added.

A cart rolled past at the end of the row, the wheels turning steadily, then stopping as someone repositioned it near the tables. The sound carried briefly, then faded into the background of the room.

"They just stood there," the man said again.

The repetition settled without change.

He did not answer right away.

He let the words remain where they were, not adjusting them, not offering anything to shift them. The room continued to move around them, unchanged by the exchange.

A volunteer approached the end of the row, stopping to check a clipboard attached to one of the cots before moving on. Another followed behind, carrying a stack of towels, setting them down on a table before turning back toward the entrance.

He shifted his weight slightly, leaning back just enough to ease the pressure on the cot, then settled again. The metal frame gave a small sound, then held.

"They told me to stay here," the man said.

He nodded.

"That's what they'll keep saying," he replied.

The man's hands loosened slightly, the fingers separating just enough to shift position before coming back together. He drew in another breath, then let it out more slowly than before.

"I don't know where she is," the man said.

The words came lower this time, closer to the floor than to him.

He kept his gaze forward.

"I know," he said.

The man did not respond.

The space between them held again, not empty, but not filled with anything new. The room continued its steady movement—voices, footsteps, the opening and closing of the doors.

He did not reach for the man.

He did not move closer.

He stayed.

And let the weight of what had been said remain where it was.

He remained seated beside the man, his hands still resting on his knees, his posture unchanged as the movement of the shelter continued around them. A volunteer pushed a cart down the aisle, one wheel catching briefly against the edge of a mat before dropping back into place, the bins on top shifting with a soft plastic knock. Someone near the entrance called out another name, louder this time, then repeated it again when no one answered. The doors opened, letting in a brief rush of cooler air along with the sound of vehicles outside, then closed again, sealing the room back into its steady hum. The man beside him did not look up.

The man drew in a breath, slower now, then let it out, the movement more even than before but still held tight at the end. His hands shifted again, fingers separating slightly before coming back together, the motion smaller than earlier, less repeated. He leaned back a fraction, then forward again, settling into the same position, elbows on knees, head angled down. The cot creaked softly beneath the adjustment and then stilled. The space between them remained.

A volunteer stepped into the aisle ahead of them, stopping to check a clipboard attached to one of the cots, then marking something before moving on. Another followed behind carrying a plastic bag filled with small items—soap, toothbrushes, folded cloths—placing them one by one at the ends of occupied cots before turning back toward the entrance. The pattern repeated down the row, each placement the same, each one completed without pause.

"They said they'll update it again," the man said.

He kept his gaze forward.

"When?" he asked.

The man shook his head once, the movement small.

"Later," he said.

The word held without detail.

Across the aisle, someone stood and moved toward the tables, guided by a volunteer who placed a hand lightly at their back to steady them. A chair scraped briefly against the floor, then settled. The overhead lights did not change.

"They keep saying later," the man said.

He nodded once.

"That's how they're doing it," he said.

The man's hands pressed together once more, then loosened again, the motion slower, less forceful than before. He rubbed his thumb along the side of his hand, then stopped, letting both hands rest.

"I should be there," the man said.

The words came out low, not directed, but placed into the space between them.

He did not answer immediately.

A responder passed behind them, speaking quietly into a radio, then lowering it as they moved toward the far end of the room. The doors opened again, then closed, the cycle repeating without change.

"They told me to stay," the man added.

He nodded once.

"That's what they're going to keep telling you," he said.

The man shifted slightly on the cot, his shoulders lifting and dropping once before settling. He leaned back a fraction, then forward again, the movement contained, not fully releasing the posture he had held since they sat down.

"They don't know," the man said.

He kept his hands where they were.

"No," he said.

The man's breathing steadied further, the rise and fall of his shoulders more even now, though the tension in his hands did not fully leave. He kept his gaze down, fixed on the same spot on the floor.

A volunteer approached the end of the row, pausing to adjust a blanket that had slipped, pulling it up and smoothing it once before stepping away.

Another volunteer moved past carrying a stack of folded towels, setting them down on a nearby table before turning back toward the entrance.

"They said if she was there, she'd be on the list," the man said.

He did not respond immediately.

He let the statement remain where it was, unchanged, not corrected, not softened. The room continued its steady movement—voices, footsteps, the rolling of carts, the opening and closing of the doors.

The man's hands loosened again, the fingers separating slightly before resting against his knees. He drew in another breath, then let it out slowly, the movement controlled.

"I keep thinking I missed her," the man said.

The words came out quieter than before, closer to the floor than to him.

He turned his head slightly, not fully, just enough to shift his attention without breaking the space.

"You came here," he said.

The man did not look up.

"They told me to," he said.

He nodded once.

"Yeah," he said.

The space held again.

No one interrupted.

No one stepped in.

The room continued around them, unchanged by what had been said.

A cart rolled past at the end of the row, the wheels turning steadily, then stopping as someone repositioned it near the tables. A volunteer called out another name near the entrance, then lowered their voice when there was no answer.

He kept his hands on his knees.

He did not reach out.

He did not move closer.

He sat.

The man remained beside him, his posture unchanged, his gaze still fixed downward, his breathing steady now, though the tension in his hands had not fully left.

They stayed there together.

The lists would be updated.

The doors would open again.

More people would come in.
The room would continue.
He did not say anything more.
He did not move.
He remained.
And held the space without changing it.

STORY 4

The Search That Ends

THE GRID HAD BEEN marked with flagging tape and stakes driven into the ground at measured intervals, each section laid out to be walked in parallel lines across the field. The terrain shifted as it moved outward from the road, the grass giving way to uneven patches of dirt and low brush that caught at boots and slowed the pace. A light wind moved across the area, enough to stir the taller grass but not enough to carry sound very far. Radios crackled at intervals, each transmission brief, then gone. The search held its shape.

He stood at the edge of the assigned sector, looking down the line of responders spaced out at equal distances, each one facing forward, waiting for the signal to begin. A clipboard rested against his forearm, the map clipped to it marked with coordinates and notes from earlier passes. One section had already been covered and cleared, the markings indicating where they had moved and what had been found. Nothing in that section had changed the status of the search.

"Spacing looks good," someone said to his right.

He nodded once without turning, his eyes still on the line. One responder adjusted their position by half a step, aligning with the others, then stilled again. Another lifted a hand briefly to shield their eyes from the sun, then lowered it. The formation held.

"Same pattern as before?" the voice asked.

"Same pattern," he said.

The response came without variation.

He lifted the radio from his chest and pressed the button. "Sector three, begin sweep," he said.

The words moved down the line without needing to be repeated. Each responder stepped forward at nearly the same moment, the formation shifting from stillness into motion, the spacing maintained as they advanced. Boots pressed into the ground, the grass bending underfoot, then lifting again after they passed. The line moved evenly.

He stepped forward with them, keeping his position slightly behind the center, his eyes moving left and right to track alignment as well as the ground ahead. The clipboard remained in his hand, the map angled so he could glance at it without stopping. The search required consistency more than speed. The ground did not change because they moved faster.

"Call out anything you see," he said, not raising his voice.

The responders continued forward, each one scanning the area in front of them, eyes moving in a pattern that had been set before they arrived. One stopped briefly, crouched to examine something in the grass, then stood and shook their head before continuing. Another stepped over a fallen branch, lifting their foot higher to clear it without breaking stride.

The line held.

A radio call came through from another sector, the voice faint, then clearer as it repeated. "Sector one negative," it said.

He acknowledged it with a short press of the button, then released it. The words did not change what they were doing. They marked where others had already been.

He kept his pace steady, matching the movement of the line, adjusting slightly when someone drifted too close or too far. The spacing corrected itself with small movements, no one needing to be told. The pattern had been practiced enough to hold.

A patch of ground ahead showed disturbance, the soil darker where it had been turned recently. He stepped toward it, lowering himself slightly to get a closer look without stopping the line entirely. The marks were shallow, inconsistent, not aligned with any clear track. He reached out, brushing the surface once with the back of his hand, then stood.

"Nothing," he said.

The line moved past it.

A responder to his left raised a hand briefly, then lowered it as he approached. "Just debris," they said.

He nodded once.

The wind shifted slightly, carrying a faint sound from beyond the far edge of the sector, then dropping it again. The field extended further than it appeared from the road, the terrain dipping and rising in ways that obscured distance. Visibility held only as far as the line.

"Maintain pace," he said.

The responders continued, each one advancing at the same measured speed, the distance between them holding. The search moved forward without interruption.

Another radio call came through. "Sector two negative," the voice said.

He pressed the button once in acknowledgment, then released it. The pattern repeated across the area, each sector clearing space without finding what they were there for. The map on his clipboard filled in slowly, each marked section reducing what remained.

He glanced down at it briefly, then back up.

The unmarked areas were fewer now.

He stepped over another patch of uneven ground, adjusting his footing as the soil shifted slightly under his weight. A responder ahead of him paused, crouched, then stood again, shaking their head before continuing. The motion repeated across the line in small variations, each one checking, each one moving on.

The field narrowed slightly toward the far end, the brush thickening just enough to slow movement but not stop it. The line adjusted again, spacing tightening where the terrain required it, then widening again as the ground opened.

"Stay aligned," he said.

No one responded.

They did not need to.

The search continued.

Each step covered ground that had not yet been walked.

Each section moved them closer to the end of what could be covered.

He kept his eyes forward, then down, then forward again, the pattern repeating with each step. The radio remained quiet for a moment, then crackled again with another report from a different sector. The words were the same.

Negative.

He pressed the button once in acknowledgment, then released it.

The line moved forward.

And the area left to search continued to shrink.

The line continued forward at the same measured pace, each responder maintaining position as the terrain shifted underfoot. The ground dipped slightly, then rose again, the brush thickening in patches that forced shorter steps before opening back into clearer sections. Boots pressed into softer soil where moisture had settled beneath the surface, then lifted, leaving shallow impressions that filled slowly as the grass bent back. A radio crackled at the edge of hearing, then cleared as the voice repeated. The pattern of movement did not change.

He adjusted his position by half a step, keeping himself aligned with the center of the formation while tracking the edges of the line with brief glances to either side. A responder to his right slowed momentarily, crouching to examine something partially obscured in the brush, then stood and shook their head before stepping forward again. Another lifted a branch with the toe of their boot, clearing it from the path without breaking stride. The spacing held without instruction.

"Maintain visual," he said.

The words carried down the line without requiring response. Each person continued scanning the ground ahead, their focus shifting between the immediate area and the next few steps forward. The search required repetition more than variation, each pass covering what the last might have missed. The terrain did not offer clear markers.

A section of ground ahead showed a faint depression, the soil pressed down in a pattern that did not match the surrounding area. He stepped toward it, lowering slightly to bring it into clearer view while keeping his forward motion. The edges were uneven, not a clean track, the shape disrupted by the movement of grass and small debris.

"Hold," he said.

The line slowed, not stopping completely, but compressing slightly as those nearest him adjusted their pace. He knelt, placing his hand near the edge of the depression without touching it, then shifted his position to view it from another angle. The marks were shallow, inconsistent, not leading in a clear direction.

"Probably runoff," someone said from his left.

He nodded once, then stood, brushing his hand lightly against his pant leg before stepping forward again.

"Continue," he said.

The line resumed full pace, the spacing widening again as the ground opened. A responder ahead lifted a hand briefly to signal a check, then lowered it as they moved on. The pattern repeated across the formation, each pause short, each return to movement immediate.

A radio call came through, clearer now as it cut across the open field. "Sector four negative," the voice said.

He pressed the button once in acknowledgment, then released it without speaking. The report added to the others, each one marking another section cleared without result. The map on his clipboard reflected it, the marked areas expanding while the remaining sections narrowed.

He glanced down at it briefly, then back up.

The unsearched area was now contained to a smaller section beyond the rise ahead.

He adjusted his pace slightly, matching the movement of the responders nearest him as the ground began to slope upward. The incline forced shorter steps, each one placed more carefully as loose soil shifted underfoot. A responder to his left lost footing momentarily, catching themselves with a quick adjustment before continuing. The line held.

"Watch your footing," someone called.

The words moved across the line, then settled as each person adjusted without breaking formation. The wind shifted again, carrying a faint sound from beyond the ridge, then dropping it as the terrain absorbed it. Visibility narrowed as the line approached the crest.

He lifted his gaze toward the top of the rise, then lowered it again to track the ground directly ahead. The search pattern did not change with elevation, only the pace.

"Keep spacing," he said.

The responders adjusted again, small movements correcting distance where the slope had compressed it. One stepped slightly wider, another slowed by half a step, the line reestablishing itself without stopping. The formation held.

They reached the crest and moved over it, the terrain leveling out briefly before dipping again into another section of brush and uneven ground. The field extended further than expected, the horizon shifting with each rise and fall. The remaining search area lay ahead, smaller now, but not yet closed.

A responder near the far edge of the line raised a hand, then paused, lowering themselves slightly to examine something in the grass. The movement drew his attention, and he adjusted his position to move closer while maintaining the line's forward motion.

"Hold," he said again.

The line slowed, compressing slightly as those nearest him adjusted. The responder remained crouched, one hand hovering over the ground, then pulling back before making contact.

"What do you have?" he asked.

The responder did not answer immediately, shifting position to look from another angle. The grass had been disturbed in a narrow path, the stems bent in one direction, then broken.

"Not sure," they said.

He stepped closer, lowering himself to see more clearly without fully stopping the line. The marks were different from the earlier depression—more defined, though still not clean.

He reached out, brushing the edge of the disturbance lightly with the back of his hand, then stood.

"Could be movement," he said.

The words carried a different weight than the earlier call.

The line remained compressed, waiting.

He looked ahead, tracing the direction of the bent grass as far as it could be followed before disappearing into the thicker brush.

"Continue," he said.

The responder stood, and the line resumed movement, adjusting direction slightly to follow the path where it could be seen. The formation shifted just enough to account for the change, then held again.

A radio call came through, overlapping with another, the voices briefly colliding before separating.

"Sector five negative," one said.

He acknowledged it with a short press of the button.

The pattern continued.

But the ground ahead had changed.

And the search had narrowed into something more specific.

The line adjusted to the new direction without breaking formation, each responder shifting a few degrees to follow the disturbed path where it could still be seen. The grass bent in a consistent line for several yards, then disappeared into a thicker patch of brush where the ground dipped. Boots pressed into the edge of it, then slowed as the footing changed, the soil softer and less stable beneath the surface. The spacing tightened briefly as the terrain compressed them, then widened again as they cleared it. No one spoke.

He moved slightly ahead of center now, tracking the path where it reappeared beyond the brush, his eyes moving between the ground and the responders on either side. A branch snapped underfoot somewhere along the line, the sound sharp, then gone. Another responder lifted a length of debris with the toe of their boot, turning it once before letting it fall back into place. The pattern held, but the pace had shifted, each step more deliberate than before.

"Keep it tight," he said.

The words carried just enough to adjust the line, each person narrowing their spacing without stopping. A responder to his left raised a hand briefly, then lowered it as they stepped forward, eyes fixed on the ground ahead. The disturbed grass appeared again, more defined now, the direction clearer as it cut across the natural growth of the field.

He followed it.

The line followed him.

A radio crackled at his chest, then cleared as the voice repeated. "All sectors report status," it said.

He did not answer yet.

The call was still moving across the grid, each sector responding in turn. He kept his attention on the ground, tracking the line where it dipped again, the brush closing in on both sides.

"Sector one negative," the voice said.

"Sector two negative."

The reports came one after another, each one the same, each one narrowing what remained.

He stepped over the edge of the dip and onto firmer ground, the brush thinning slightly as the terrain leveled. The disturbed path continued for several more feet, then broke apart, the marks less consistent, the direction less clear.

"Hold," he said.

The line slowed again, compressing slightly as those nearest him adjusted their pace. A responder to his right crouched, examining the ground more closely, then shifted position to look from another angle. Another stepped back half a step to maintain spacing, then stilled.

He lowered himself slightly, bringing his line of sight closer to the ground without fully kneeling. The marks were there, but less defined now, the grass bent in multiple directions, the soil disturbed in patches rather than a single line.

"Losing it," someone said quietly.

He did not respond.

He moved a few steps forward, scanning for where the pattern might pick up again, his eyes tracing the ground in a widening arc. A responder to his left mirrored the movement, stepping outward slightly, then pausing.

"Nothing here," they said.

The line held.

No one advanced.

He straightened, looking ahead.

The remaining search area stretched out in front of them, smaller now, contained between two natural boundaries where the terrain rose and the brush thickened. The grid had been narrowed to this final section.

The radio crackled again.

"Sector three status," the voice said.

He pressed the button.

"Sector three following possible track," he said. "Continuing."

"Copy," the voice answered.

He released the button and looked back down at the ground.

The marks were still there, but not enough to define a clear direction.

He stepped forward again.

The line followed.

Each responder moved into the space ahead, scanning the ground with renewed focus, the pattern widening slightly to compensate for the loss of a clear path. Boots pressed into the soil, then lifted, leaving shallow impressions that overlapped as they moved.

A responder near the far edge of the line stopped, crouched, then raised a hand.

"Hold," they called.

The word moved across the formation, each person stopping in place, the line freezing where it stood. The wind moved through the grass, bending it in small waves that passed and then settled.

He turned and moved toward the responder, stepping carefully between the others to avoid breaking the spacing more than necessary. The responder remained crouched, one hand hovering over the ground, then pulling back before making contact.

"What do you have?" he asked.

The responder shifted slightly, angling their body to give him a clearer view.

"There," they said.

He lowered himself beside them.

The ground showed a deeper disturbance here, the soil pressed down more firmly, the grass flattened in a wider area. It did not match the earlier marks.

He reached out, brushing the edge lightly with the back of his hand, then moved his hand away.

The impression held.

He looked closer.

The shape was not clean.

But it was not random.

He stood.

"Mark it," he said.

A responder stepped forward, placing a flag at the edge of the disturbed area, the bright color standing out against the ground. Another took a step back to maintain spacing as the line adjusted around the marker.

He looked ahead again.

The remaining section lay just beyond.

"Continue," he said.

The line moved forward once more, stepping past the marker, the formation reestablishing itself as they advanced into the final area.

The radio remained quiet.

The wind moved lightly across the field.

And the space left to search was almost gone.

The line moved past the marker and reformed without stopping, each responder stepping back into position as the spacing corrected itself across the narrowing field. The terrain leveled briefly, then dipped again into a shallow basin where the grass grew thicker and the ground held more moisture beneath the surface. Boots pressed deeper here, leaving clearer impressions before lifting, the soil clinging slightly before releasing. The wind dropped as the terrain enclosed them, the sound of movement carrying more clearly within the space. No one spoke.

He shifted his position back toward the center of the line, letting the responders on either side reestablish the edges of the formation. The flagged disturbance remained behind them, visible for a few steps before the rise obscured it from view. A responder to his left adjusted their spacing by half a step, then steadied, their gaze fixed on the ground ahead. Another lifted a section of flattened grass with the toe of their boot, then let it fall back without pausing.

"Maintain alignment," he said.

The words moved across the line without response, each person adjusting slightly where needed. The pattern held, though the pace had slowed again, each step placed with more care as the ground softened. A radio crackled faintly, then cleared as the transmission repeated from another sector.

"Sector five negative," the voice said.

He acknowledged it with a short press of the button, then lowered the radio without speaking. The report added to the others, each one narrowing the remaining area to the section directly in front of them.

The basin closed slightly as they moved further in, the edges rising on either side, limiting visibility beyond the line itself. The grass stood higher here, brushing against boots and pant legs, bending and then lifting again as they passed. The ground showed more signs of disturbance—patches where the surface had been pressed down, then partially lifted again.

"Check carefully," he said.

A responder to his right crouched briefly, brushing aside a section of grass with their hand, then stood and shook their head before continuing. Another paused for a moment longer, tracing a shallow impression with their eyes before stepping forward again. The line compressed slightly, then widened again as they cleared the thicker section.

He moved forward, scanning the ground in overlapping arcs, his gaze shifting between the immediate area and the few steps ahead. The disturbed patches appeared more frequently now, though none held a clear shape or direction. The pattern suggested movement, but not enough to define it.

A responder near the center of the line slowed, then stopped, raising a hand.

"Hold," they said.

The word carried quickly, the formation stopping in place, each person freezing where they stood. The wind moved lightly across the basin, bending the taller grass in small waves before settling again. The sound of breathing, of shifting weight, of fabric moving against fabric, became more noticeable in the absence of forward motion.

He stepped toward the responder, moving between the others without breaking the spacing more than necessary. The responder remained still, one foot slightly forward, their gaze fixed on the ground.

"What do you have?" he asked.

The responder pointed without stepping closer.

"There," they said.

He followed the line of their gesture.

The ground showed a deeper indentation than the surrounding area, the grass flattened in a wider shape, the soil beneath pressed down more firmly. The edges were uneven, but the center held.

He stepped closer, lowering himself slightly to see the shape more clearly. The indentation did not match the earlier disturbances. It held weight.

He reached out, brushing the edge lightly with the back of his hand, then pulled away. The grass did not spring back immediately.

He stood.

"Mark it," he said.

A responder stepped forward with a flag, placing it at the edge of the indentation, the color bright against the muted ground. Another adjusted their position to maintain spacing as the line shifted around the marker.

He looked ahead.

The remaining section of the basin extended only a short distance further, bounded by a rise that closed the field beyond. The area left to search had narrowed to a final stretch.

"Continue," he said.

The line stepped forward again, moving past the marker, the formation reestablishing itself as they advanced. Each responder scanned the ground with the same pattern, the movement steady but slower now, the spacing tighter within the enclosed space.

A radio call came through, clearer within the basin.

"All sectors report status," the voice said.

He did not answer yet.

The call moved across the grid, each sector responding in turn, the reports overlapping briefly before separating into distinct transmissions.

"Sector one negative."

"Sector two negative."

"Sector four negative."

He lifted the radio, then lowered it again, his attention still on the ground ahead.

The basin ended just beyond the next rise.

The remaining area was almost gone.

He stepped forward.

The line followed.

And the search moved into its final section.

The line moved up the last rise together, the spacing tightening slightly as the slope forced shorter steps and closer alignment. Boots pressed into the softer soil near the base, then onto firmer ground as they climbed, the surface leveling at the top before dropping away on the far side. The grass thinned near the crest, giving way to patches of exposed dirt and scattered debris that had collected along the incline. The wind returned as they cleared the rise, moving across the open space beyond. No one spoke.

He stepped onto the flat ground and slowed, letting the line reestablish its spacing across the final section. The remaining area stretched out in front of them, smaller now, contained by the boundaries they had already cleared. A responder to his left adjusted position by half a step, then steadied, their gaze fixed downward. Another lifted a piece of debris with the toe of their boot, turned it once, then set it aside without stopping. The formation held.

"Final sweep," he said.

The words carried across the line, quiet but clear. Each responder stepped forward, the movement uniform, the spacing maintained as they advanced into the last section of the grid. The ground showed signs of earlier disturbance—patches where grass had been flattened, soil pressed down—but no clear pattern remained. The search moved through it without breaking stride.

A radio crackled at his chest.

"All sectors prepare to report," the voice said.

He did not answer.

He kept his eyes on the ground, tracking each step, each section as it passed beneath the line. A responder ahead slowed briefly, crouched to examine something in the dirt, then stood and shook their head before continuing. Another paused for half a step, then resumed, the movement barely interrupting the line.

"Stay aligned," he said.

The responders adjusted slightly, correcting spacing where needed, the formation holding steady. The distance between them remained consistent, each person covering their section without overlap.

The ground ahead leveled into a shallow clearing, the grass shorter here, the soil more exposed. The visibility improved, the line extending further across the space without obstruction. The final section narrowed to a strip no wider than the formation itself.

A responder near the far edge of the line stopped.

Raised a hand.

"Hold," they said.

The word carried across the line, each person stopping where they stood, the formation freezing in place. The wind moved lightly across the clearing, lifting small fragments of debris, then letting them fall again.

He turned and moved toward the responder, stepping carefully between the others, his eyes fixed on the point where the hand had been raised. The responder remained still, one foot slightly forward, their gaze directed downward.

"What do you have?" he asked.

The responder shifted slightly, stepping back just enough to give him space.

"There," they said.

He stepped forward.

The ground showed a clear indentation, deeper than the others, the soil pressed down in a defined shape. The grass around it had been flattened outward, the pattern consistent with weight and movement. It did not match the scattered disturbances they had passed earlier.

He lowered himself slightly, bringing his line of sight closer without fully kneeling. The edges held.

He reached out, brushing the surface lightly with the back of his hand, then withdrew it.

The impression remained.

He stood.

"Mark it," he said.

A responder stepped forward with a flag, placing it at the edge of the indentation, the bright color standing out against the ground. Another moved to adjust spacing as the line shifted around the marker.

He looked ahead.

There was no ground left beyond.

He turned slightly, letting his gaze move across the width of the formation, tracking each responder from one edge of the line to the other. The ground behind them showed the path they had taken, faint impressions of boots crossing and recrossing the field, overlapping patterns where each section had been walked. Flags marked the earlier disturbances at intervals, small points of color against the flattened grass. No section remained unbroken.

He lifted the radio.

"All sectors report," the voice said.

"Sector three," he said. "Final section complete. One area marked for follow-up."

"Copy," the voice answered.

He lowered the radio.

The responders remained where they were, the line no longer moving, the formation holding without direction. One shifted their weight from one foot to the other, then stilled again. Another lowered their gaze further, scanning the ground out of habit, though there was nothing left to cover.

He looked once more across the field.

From one boundary to the other, the grid had been walked, the ground marked by their passage, each section accounted for. The markers stood where they had been placed, and the rest of the field lay empty of anything new.

"Stand down," he said.

The words moved across the formation, quiet but final. The responders lowered their hands, some stepping back half a step, others turning slightly where they stood. The line broke without disorder, the spacing dissolving into smaller movements.

A responder pulled the flag slightly to ensure it held in place, then stepped back. Another turned toward the direction they had come from, adjusting their footing on the uneven ground.

He remained where he was for a moment longer, his gaze still on the marked area, the indentation unchanged, the flag steady against the wind.

The radio remained quiet.

The field held.

The search had ended.

And the work that remained was no longer theirs.

The Weight

STORY 5

The Call They Didn't Send

The phones sat in a row along the folding table, each one plugged into a power strip that ran the length of the wall and disappeared behind a stack of boxes at the far end. Chargers crossed over each other in loose loops, some taped down where they had been pulled free too many times. A laptop sat open near the center, the screen filled with a spreadsheet that scrolled as someone moved through it, names shifting upward in small increments. The room was quieter than the shelter, but not still—voices stayed low, contained, each one held close to the person speaking. The door opened and closed at intervals, letting in brief noise from the hallway before settling again.

He stood at the edge of the table, one hand resting near a stack of printed sheets, the other holding his phone without looking at it. A volunteer sat across from him, head tilted slightly toward the screen, one hand on the keyboard, the other holding a pen that tapped once against the table before stopping. A list lay between them, names arranged in columns, notes written in the margins where updates had come in. Some lines were marked with check marks, others left blank.

"Still waiting on confirmation for these," the volunteer said, tapping the edge of the page with the pen.

He leaned slightly closer, scanning the names without touching the paper. The print was small, the lines tight, the spacing reduced to fit more onto each page. A few names had been crossed out and rewritten, corrections made in handwriting that did not match the original print.

"How long?" he asked.

The volunteer glanced at the laptop, then back to the page.

"Since this morning," they said.

The answer came without emphasis.

He straightened, letting his hand fall back to his side. Another phone vibrated against the table, the sound brief, then stopping as someone picked it up and answered quietly. The conversation stayed low, the words not carrying beyond the immediate space.

"Any updates from the field?" he asked.

The volunteer shook their head once, eyes returning to the screen.

"Nothing new," they said.

A line on the spreadsheet moved up as they scrolled, the names shifting again. One column showed status, another location, a third left empty where information had not yet been entered. The empty spaces outnumbered the filled ones.

He picked up one of the printed sheets, holding it at the edge rather than lifting it fully, scanning the section that had been marked earlier. A name near the middle had been circled, a note written beside it in darker ink.

"Who's handling this one?" he asked.

The volunteer leaned closer, following his line of sight.

"Was assigned earlier," they said. "Waiting on callback."

He nodded once.

A phone rang at the far end of the table, louder than the others, then stopped as it was answered. The person who picked it up turned slightly away from the table, their voice lowering as they spoke. Another volunteer moved past behind him, carrying a stack of folders, placing them down near the laptop before stepping back.

He set the sheet down again, aligning it with the others without pressing it into place. The edges of the pages did not match exactly, the stack uneven where it had been handled repeatedly.

"Have we tried again?" he asked.

The volunteer paused, their hand resting on the keyboard.

"Not yet," they said.

The answer held for a moment.

"Why not?" he asked.

The volunteer looked at the screen, then back at the page.

"We were told to wait," they said.

The words were delivered the same way as the others—without emphasis, without explanation beyond what had been given.

He shifted his weight slightly, adjusting his stance where he stood. The floor beneath him was solid, the movement minimal, but enough to register.

"Who said that?" he asked.

The volunteer glanced toward the far end of the room, then back.

"Command," they said.

He nodded once.

The laptop screen refreshed, the spreadsheet updating as a new line appeared near the bottom. The volunteer's hand moved to the trackpad, scrolling again, the names shifting upward once more.

A phone vibrated again near his hand, the screen lighting briefly before dimming. He did not pick it up.

"Any reason given?" he asked.

The volunteer shook their head.

"No," they said.

Another call came in, this one answered immediately by someone further down the table. The voice on the other end was louder, carrying enough that a few words could be heard—location, time, unclear—before the volunteer lowered their voice again and turned away.

He looked back at the circled name.

The ink had bled slightly into the paper, the edges of the circle uneven where the pen had pressed harder in one place than another. The note beside it had been written quickly, the letters compressed.

"Who made the first contact?" he asked.

The volunteer checked the sheet again.

"Field unit," they said. "They flagged it."

He nodded.

"And we haven't called since?"

The volunteer hesitated, their hand lifting slightly from the keyboard before settling again.

"No," they said.

The answer remained.

He placed his hand flat on the table, not pressing, just resting it there near the edge of the page. The surface was smooth, the paper shifting slightly under his fingers.

"Phone number's here?" he asked.

The volunteer nodded, pointing to a line beneath the name.

"Right there."

He followed the line with his eyes, reading the number without saying it aloud. The digits sat in a column that had been partially filled, some entries complete, others missing entirely.

A chair scraped lightly against the floor as someone stood, then moved away from the table. The door opened again, a brief rush of hallway noise entering before closing once more.

He did not reach for the phone.

He did not pick up the sheet.

He stood where he was, his hand still resting near the name.

The room continued around him—phones ringing, voices low, names shifting on the screen.

The line remained unmarked.

And the call had not been made.

He kept his hand resting nearthe edge of the page, his fingers lightly touching the paper without pressing it flat. The volunteer across from him shifted slightly in their chair, the legs scraping softly against the floor before settling again. The laptop screen refreshed, a new line appearing near the bottom of the spreadsheet, then sliding upward as the list adjusted. A phone rang twice near the center of the table before being answered, the voice that followed kept low and close.

"Is this still assigned?" he asked.

The volunteer looked at the sheet, then at the screen, their hand moving between the two without fully committing to either. The pen tapped once against the table, then stopped.

"Yeah," they said. "Still assigned."

"To who?" he asked.

The volunteer scrolled, eyes moving quickly across the rows, then stopping as they found the entry. They leaned in closer, reading, then straightened slightly.

"Team B," they said.

He nodded once.

"Where are they now?"

The volunteer hesitated, their hand hovering over the keyboard before typing something quickly, then stopping. The screen shifted again, the row moving upward as more names were entered below.

"Out in sector four," they said. "Last check-in about an hour ago."

He looked back at the circled name.

The ink had dried, but the edges of the circle still held uneven where the pen had pressed harder in places. The number beneath it remained unchanged, the digits clear against the page.

"They were supposed to call?" he asked.

The volunteer nodded.

"That was the plan," they said.

Another phone rang at the far end of the table, the sound sharper this time, then cut off as it was answered. The volunteer who picked it up turned away slightly, one hand covering the other ear to hear more clearly. A second voice rose briefly, then lowered again.

"And they didn't?" he asked.

The volunteer shook their head once.

"No."

The answer came without elaboration.

He shifted his weight slightly, the movement small but enough to change his stance. The table edge pressed lightly against his thigh, then eased as he adjusted.

"Did anyone follow up?" he asked.

The volunteer looked at the screen again, then back at the paper, their eyes moving between the two as if expecting something to appear that had not been entered.

"No," they said.

The word held.

A chair moved behind him, the legs scraping once before lifting and setting down again in a new position. Someone crossed the room carrying a stack of folders, placing them near the far end of the table before stepping back. The door opened, then closed, the hallway noise briefly filling the space before fading.

"We were told to wait," the volunteer added.

He nodded once.

"For what?" he asked.

The volunteer paused, their hand resting flat on the table now instead of the keyboard.

"Confirmation," they said.

"From where?"

"From the field," they said.

The exchange settled.

He looked again at the number.

The digits did not change.

The line did not update.

Another phone vibrated near his hand, the screen lighting briefly before dimming again. He did not pick it up.

"How long do we wait?" he asked.

The volunteer did not answer immediately.

They glanced toward the far end of the room, where another group sat with their own set of lists, their voices even lower, their movements slower. One of them leaned back in their chair, rubbing their eyes before returning to the screen in front of them.

"They didn't say," the volunteer replied.

The words carried the same tone as before—flat, without emphasis, without interpretation.

He moved his hand slightly, lifting it from the table and then setting it back down a few inches closer to the circled name. The paper shifted under the motion, the edges sliding against the stack beneath it.

"And if it doesn't come?" he asked.

The volunteer looked at him briefly, then back at the page.

"We wait," they said.

The answer remained.

A phone rang again, closer this time, the sound cutting through the lower voices before being answered. The volunteer who picked it up spoke quickly, then slowed, listening, their head turning slightly as they tried to hear over the room.

He looked across the table.

The laptop screen continued to move, names shifting upward, new entries appearing at the bottom. Some lines filled in, others remained blank. The column marked "contact" showed scattered entries, some marked complete, others empty.

The circled name remained in the middle.

Unchanged.

He reached toward the phone nearest him, his fingers hovering just above it without making contact. The screen lit briefly again, then dimmed, the device still.

The volunteer watched his hand for a moment, then looked back at the screen.

"We were told to wait," they said again.

He did not respond.

He let his hand remain where it was, suspended above the phone, not moving closer, not pulling away. The room continued around them—phones ringing, voices low, the steady movement of names across the screen.

The number remained on the page.

The line remained open.

And the call still had not been made.

His hand hovered above the phone for a moment longer, then lowered slightly, stopping just short of touching the screen. The device remained still on the table, its surface reflecting the overhead lights in a dull sheen. Across from him, the volunteer shifted in their chair, adjusting their position as the laptop screen refreshed again, the rows of names sliding upward in small increments. A pen rolled a few inches across the table, then stopped against the edge of a stack of papers. The room held its steady rhythm.

"Do we have anyone else assigned to this?" he asked.

The volunteer looked back at the sheet, then at the screen, their eyes moving quickly between the two. Their hand moved to the keyboard, typing briefly, then pausing as the cursor blinked in place.

"No," they said. "Just that team."

He nodded once.

"And they haven't checked back in?"

The volunteer shook their head.

"Not on this one."

A phone rang near the far end of the table, louder than the others, then cut off as it was answered. The volunteer who picked it up turned slightly away, one hand pressed against the other ear, their voice dropping lower as they spoke. Another responder crossed behind them, carrying a binder, setting it down near the laptop before stepping back.

He lowered his hand the rest of the way to the table, placing it beside the phone rather than on it. His fingers rested against the surface, not moving.

"When was the last attempt?" he asked.

The volunteer scanned the page again, tracing a line with the tip of the pen before stopping.

"Earlier this morning," they said. "First contact attempt."

"And nothing since?"

"No."

The answer remained.

The laptop screen refreshed again, a new entry appearing near the bottom, then shifting upward as more lines were added. One of the columns filled in with a check mark, another remained blank. The cursor moved, then stopped.

He looked back at the circled name.

The ink had set into the paper, the line of the circle uneven but fixed. The number beneath it remained unchanged, the digits clear and complete.

"They're expecting us to wait for them to call it in?" he asked.

The volunteer nodded once.

"That's what we were told."

"Even if it doesn't come?"

The volunteer hesitated, their hand lifting slightly from the keyboard before settling again.

"They said wait," they repeated.

The words held the same shape as before.

A chair shifted behind him, the legs scraping lightly as someone stood and moved toward the door. The handle turned, the door opening just enough to let in a brief rush of hallway noise before closing again. The room returned to its steady hum.

He moved his hand slightly, sliding it closer to the phone, then stopping again. The screen remained dark.

"Is there a protocol for this?" he asked.

The volunteer looked at him briefly, then back at the screen.

"There is," they said.

"What does it say?"

They turned slightly, pulling a binder closer from the edge of the table. The cover bent as they opened it, flipping through a few pages before stopping. Their finger traced a line down the page, then paused.

"Wait for field confirmation before making secondary contact," they read.

He nodded once.

"How long?" he asked.

The volunteer scanned further down the page, then shook their head.

"Doesn't say," they replied.

The binder remained open for a moment longer, then was closed and set back down, the edge of it resting against the stack of printed sheets.

He looked again at the number.

The digits did not change.

The line did not fill.

A phone vibrated again near his hand, the screen lighting briefly before dimming. He did not reach for it.

"What happens if we call anyway?" he asked.

The volunteer did not answer immediately.

They looked at him, then at the page, then back at the screen, their hand resting still on the keyboard.

"We weren't told to do that," they said.

The answer held.

Across the table, another volunteer leaned forward, speaking quietly into a phone, then listening, their expression unchanged as they nodded once and wrote something down. The pen moved quickly, then stopped.

He shifted his stance slightly, the movement small but enough to change the angle of his weight. The edge of the table pressed lightly against his leg, then eased.

The phone remained where it was.

The number remained on the page.

The binder sat closed.

The laptop continued to update.

He lifted his hand again, this time placing his fingers lightly against the edge of the phone, not picking it up, just making contact. The surface was cool, unmoving.

Across from him, the volunteer watched the movement, then looked back at the screen.

"We were told to wait," they said again.

He did not answer.

He let his hand rest against the phone, his fingers still, not pressing, not lifting.

The room continued around him—calls answered, names entered, pages shifted, voices low.

The instruction remained.

The number remained.

And the call still had not been made.

His fingers rested against the edge of the phone, the device unmoving beneath them as the screen stayed dark. He did not pick it up. Across from him, the volunteer shifted slightly in their chair, one hand returning to the keyboard as the spreadsheet refreshed again, rows sliding upward as new entries appeared below. A pen tapped once against the table, then stopped, the sound brief and contained. The room continued at the same low level—voices close, phones answered quickly, movement steady but controlled.

A phone rang near the far end of the table, louder than the others, then cut off as it was answered. The volunteer who picked it up turned away, one hand cupped over the receiver, their voice dropping further as they spoke. Another responder stepped in behind them, waiting for space at the table, a folder held against their side. The door opened and closed again, the hallway noise entering and then disappearing just as quickly.

"Do we log this as pending?" he asked.

The volunteer glanced at the screen, then back at the printed sheet, their eyes moving between the two.

"It already is," they said.

"Anything added since this morning?"

The volunteer shook their head once.

"No updates."

The answer settled without change.

He shifted his hand slightly on the table, the edge of his palm brushing against the phone before resting again just beside it. The device remained still, the screen unlit. The number on the page remained where it had been, unchanged, the ink settled into the paper.

"Who else knows about this one?" he asked.

The volunteer looked toward the far end of the room, then back again.

"Command," they said. "And the field team."

He nodded once.

"No one else?"

The volunteer shook their head.

"No."

A chair scraped lightly behind him as someone stood and moved toward the door, pausing briefly before stepping out into the hallway. The sound of their footsteps faded as the door closed again.

He looked back at the circled name.

The edges of the ink had darkened slightly where the pen had pressed harder, the line uneven but fixed. The note beside it remained compressed, written quickly, not revisited.

"What was the note?" he asked.

The volunteer leaned forward slightly, reading from the page.

"'Possible contact. Needs confirmation,'" they said.

He nodded.

"That was this morning?"

"Yes."

The laptop screen refreshed again, a new entry appearing near the bottom, then shifting upward as more names were added. One column filled in with a check mark, another remained blank. The cursor blinked, then moved.

He kept his gaze on the page.

"Has anyone tried to verify it another way?" he asked.

The volunteer hesitated, their hand resting flat on the table now instead of the keyboard.

"No," they said.

The word held.

A phone vibrated again near his hand, the screen lighting briefly before dimming. He did not pick it up.

"Is there anything preventing us from calling?" he asked.

The volunteer looked at him, then back at the screen, their hand lifting slightly before settling again.

"We were told to wait," they said.

The answer came the same way as before.

He did not respond.

He let his hand remain where it was, close to the phone, not touching it now, the space between his fingers and the device small but unchanged.

Across the table, another volunteer leaned forward, speaking quietly into a phone, then nodding once as they listened. They wrote something down, the pen moving quickly, then set it aside.

The room continued—phones ringing, voices low, names shifting across the screen.

He looked again at the number.

The digits did not move.

The line did not fill.

The instruction remained.

"Is there a time when we stop waiting?" he asked.

The volunteer did not answer immediately.

They looked at the screen, then at the page, then back at him, their expression unchanged.

"No," they said.

The word settled.

A cart rolled past the doorway, the wheels audible for a moment before fading. Someone called out for a name near the far end of the room, then repeated it again when there was no response.

He shifted his weight slightly, the movement small, the edge of the table pressing lightly against his leg before easing again.

His hand remained near the phone.

The volunteer returned their attention to the screen, typing briefly, then stopping as the cursor moved.

The list continued to change.

The circled name did not.

The number remained.

And the call still had not been made.

His hand remained near the phone, not touching it now, the space between his fingers and the edge of the device unchanged. The screen stayed dark. Across from him, the volunteer leaned forward again, typing briefly, then stopping as the spreadsheet refreshed, rows shifting upward in small increments. A new name appeared near the bottom, then moved as another entry was added beneath it. The pen beside the keyboard rolled slightly, then settled against the laptop.

A phone rang near the center of the table, the sound sharp, then cut off as it was answered. The volunteer who picked it up spoke quietly, turning their body away to hear more clearly, one hand pressed against the other ear. Another responder stepped into the space they left, setting down a folder, opening it, and scanning the first page without sitting.

He looked back at the circled name.

The ink had not changed.

The number remained clear beneath it.

The note beside it—"Possible contact. Needs confirmation."—sat where it had been written hours earlier, the letters compressed into the margin.

He shifted his stance slightly, the movement small, the edge of the table pressing lightly against his thigh before easing again. His hand lifted a fraction, then lowered again without reaching for the phone.

"Any new field reports?" he asked.

The volunteer shook their head without looking up.

"Nothing on this," they said.

The answer held.

The laptop screen refreshed again, a new column filling in for another entry, a check mark appearing where there had been none. The cursor blinked, then moved to the next line.

He watched it for a moment, then looked back at the page.

The circled name remained in the same position.

Unmoved.

A chair shifted behind him as someone sat down, the legs scraping once before settling. The door opened, a brief rush of hallway noise entering, then closed again, returning the room to its contained hum.

"Has anyone from command checked this specifically?" he asked.

The volunteer paused, their hands resting on the keyboard.

"I don't know," they said.

The answer did not extend further.

A phone vibrated again near his hand, the screen lighting briefly before dimming. He did not reach for it.

He looked at the number again.

Read it once more without speaking.

The digits held.

Across the table, a volunteer finished a call, set the phone down, and immediately reached for another sheet, scanning it before picking up a pen. The motion was continuous, the transition from one task to the next without pause.

He placed his hand flat on the table again, closer now to the phone than before, but still not touching it. The surface beneath his palm was smooth, the paper shifting slightly under the edge of his hand.

"If they don't call it in," he said, "does it stay like this?"

The volunteer looked at him, then back at the screen.

"Yes," they said.

The word landed without emphasis.

He nodded once.

The laptop updated again, the rows shifting upward, the list continuing to move. Another name appeared near the bottom, then another, the entries filling in as information came in from elsewhere.

The circled name did not move.

The column beside it remained blank.

A phone rang again, then another, the sounds overlapping briefly before being answered. Voices rose slightly, then lowered again, each conversation contained within its own space.

He lifted his hand once more, this time placing his fingers lightly against the phone, the contact brief, then resting there. The device did not move.

Across from him, the volunteer watched for a moment, then returned their gaze to the screen.

"We were told to wait," they said.

He did not answer.

He left his hand where it was, resting against the phone, not lifting it, not dialing.

The room continued—calls answered, names entered, lists updated.

The instruction held.

The number remained.

The line stayed open.

He withdrew his hand from the phone and let it rest back on the table beside the page, the movement small, contained. The device remained where it was, the screen dark.

Across the table, the spreadsheet shifted again, the rows continuing to move upward, the bottom filling, the top disappearing.

The circled name remained in place.

No check mark.

No note added.

No change.

He looked at it once more, then lifted his gaze slightly toward the rest of the room, tracking the movement of volunteers, the phones, the lists, the steady flow of information that did not include this line.

He did not reach for the phone again.

He did not speak.

He stood where he was.

And the call was not made.

STORY 6

The Volunteer Who Stayed Too Long

THE REGISTRATION TABLE SAT along the side wall where the gym narrowed slightly, two folding tables pushed together and covered with clipboards, stacks of forms, and loose pens that had been used and set down wherever there was space. A strip of blue tape ran along the floor in front of it, marking where people were supposed to stop, though the line pressed past it in places where the room filled faster than it could be managed. The overhead lights stayed fixed at full brightness, flattening the space so there were no shadows to mark time. A low current of voices moved through the room, interrupted by the occasional scrape of a chair or the rolling of a cart.

She stood behind the table with one foot slightly forward, bracing herself against the edge as her hand moved across the form in front of her. The pen did not stop except to shift lines, the motion practiced enough that she did not need to look down at every word she wrote. To her left, astack of completed forms leaned slightly, the top pages slipping out of alignment until another volunteer reached over to tap them flat. To her right, a fresh stack waited, edges squared, the top page already pulled halfway forward for the next entry.

"Next," she said.

A man stepped forward, stopping just short of the tape before being motioned closer by the volunteer beside her. He held a folded paper in both hands, the edges softened from being handled repeatedly, and placed it on the table without speaking. She drew it toward her with two fingers, smoothing it once against the surface before setting it aside and pulling a blank form into place. The motion was continuous, one page replaced by another without pause.

"Name?" she asked.

He answered, his voice low but steady, and she wrote it down immediately, the pen moving without hesitation. She shifted to the next line before the ink had fully dried, her hand already moving as she asked the next question. The man adjusted his stance slightly, one foot sliding back as the line pressed forward behind him.

"Address?"

He gave it, slower this time, and she leaned just enough to hear without asking him to repeat it. The pen continued across the page, filling the space even where his answer came in pieces. She marked a box, then moved to the next line.

"Anyone with you?"

"No," he said.

She checked the space and slid the form toward him, pointing briefly to the line where he needed to sign. He did, his hand pausing once before finishing, then stepped aside as the next person moved into place. She did not watch him leave.

"Next."

A woman stepped forward holding a small bag against her side, her shoulders drawn inward as she approached the table. She set the bag down near her feet before stepping closer, her fingers resting lightly on the edge of the table as if testing whether it would hold. The volunteer beside her shifted a stack of forms to make space without interrupting the movement of the line.

"Name?" she asked.

The woman answered, her voice quieter than the man before her, and she leaned slightly forward to catch it, her pen already moving as the words came. The line behind the woman compressed, two people stepping closer together to close the gap left at the front. Somewhere behind them, a phone rang, then stopped as it was picked up.

"Address?"

The woman hesitated, her eyes dropping briefly to the table before she spoke. She wrote the response as it came, not waiting for it to settle into a full sentence, filling the line as the words formed. The pen pressed harder for a moment, then eased.

"Anyone with you?"

The woman shook her head.

She marked the box and slid the form forward, tapping once near the signature line. The woman signed, her hand unsteady, then picked up the bag and stepped aside as the next person moved forward. The space at the front closed immediately.

"Next."

The word came without change.

A volunteer behind her set a bottle of water near the edge of the table within her reach, the plastic making a soft sound as it touched the surface. She did not look at it. The condensation on the bottle began to collect and run down the side, forming a small ring where it met the table.

A man stepped forward, his jacket folded over one arm, his other hand empty and unsure where to rest. He looked down at the form, then at her hand as it moved, then back to the form again. The line behind him shifted again, someone stepping out briefly before returning to place.

"Name?" she asked.

He answered, and she wrote it down without lifting her pen, her hand moving in the same steady rhythm. She shifted to the next line before he had fully finished speaking, catching the end of his answer as it came.

"Address?"

He hesitated, then gave it.

She wrote, then checked a box, then moved to the next line.

"Anyone with you?"

He shook his head.

She marked the space and pushed the form toward him, her finger landing briefly on the line where he needed to sign. He did, then stepped aside, his jacket slipping slightly before he adjusted it again. She did not look up.

"Next."

The line moved.

A volunteer leaned in beside her, speaking quietly, too low for the words to carry, then straightened when she nodded once without breaking her movement. Another volunteer lifted a portion of the completed stack and carried it toward the laptop table across the room, where names were being entered into a spreadsheet that shifted constantly as new lines were added.

She shifted her weight slightly, her knee bending just enough to relieve the pressure, then straightened again without stepping away from the table. The pen continued to move across the page, the motion unchanged.

"Next," she said.

Another person stepped forward.

She did not look up.

She did not slow.

The line continued to move.

And she remained at the table.

The line tightened again as more people moved in from the entrance, the space behind the tape filling until the boundary stopped meaning anything except where the table began. A volunteer at the end of the row raised a hand and called for spacing, guiding two people back half a step before turning to receive another group coming through the doors. The sound of movement shifted with it—bags set down, shoes scraping, voices rising briefly before lowering again. The table remained the fixed point where everything narrowed.

She pulled the next form forward before the previous one had fully cleared the space, aligning it with the edge of the table using the side of her hand. The pen stayed in motion, the tip catching slightly on a crease in the paper before smoothing out as she adjusted pressure. To her right, the stack of blank forms had lowered by nearly half, the top page already bent where she had drawn it forward in preparation. To her left, the completed stack was lifted again and divided into two, one portion carried away, the other tapped into alignment and set back down.

"Next," she said.

A man stepped forward carrying a small duffel bag, the strap looped twice around his wrist. He placed it on the floor with a soft thud, then rested his hand briefly on the table before pulling it back as if unsure whether he should touch anything. His eyes moved across the forms, then settled on her hand as it wrote.

"Name?" she asked.

He answered, and she wrote it immediately, the letters forming without pause. She shifted to the next line before he had finished speaking, catching the last syllables as they came. The pen did not lift.

"Address?"

He hesitated, glancing toward the line behind him as it pressed forward, then gave the answer in shorter pieces. She filled the line as the words came, leaving no gap where the pause had been.

"Anyone with you?"

He shook his head once.

She marked the box and slid the form toward him, her finger landing near the signature line before lifting again. He signed, the pen pressing harder than hers had, then stepped aside, lifting the duffel bag without fully looking up. The next person moved in before he cleared the space.

"Next."

A woman stepped forward with a child at her side, the child holding onto the edge of her coat and leaning slightly behind her leg. She guided the child forward with a small motion of her hand, then placed both hands on the table as if to steady herself. The volunteer beside the table shifted a clipboard out of the way to make space.

"Name?" she asked.

The woman answered, her voice quieter than the surrounding movement, and she leaned forward just enough to catch it, her pen already moving. The line behind them compressed again, someone stepping sideways to make room for another person entering from the doors.

"Address?"

The woman paused, her grip tightening briefly on the edge of the table before she spoke. She wrote as the words came, not waiting for them to settle into a full phrase. The pen pressed slightly deeper for a moment, then eased again.

"Anyone with you?"

The woman gestured toward the child.

She marked the space and added a note in the margin, the line shorter and more compressed than the others. The child stepped closer when motioned, their hand still gripping the coat.

She slid the form forward and tapped once at the signature line. The woman signed, guiding the paper with one hand while keeping the other near the child's shoulder, then stepped aside. The space filled immediately.

"Next."

The word came the same.

A volunteer reached across the table and moved the bottle of water closer to her hand, the base leaving a thin ring where condensation had collected. The plastic shifted slightly as it was set down, then stilled. She did not look at it.

"You need to rotate out," the volunteer said, low enough that it did not carry past the table.

She did not pause.

"I'm fine," she said.

The pen continued across the page, the motion unchanged.

The volunteer remained for a moment, watching her hand as it moved, then reached for the completed stack instead, lifting it and carrying it toward the data table without saying anything further.

"Next," she said.

A man stepped forward, then stopped, his gaze fixed on the form before speaking. His hands hovered near the edge of the table, then pulled back, then returned again as if he had not decided where they belonged. The line behind him shifted, someone stepping forward too quickly before correcting themselves.

"Name?" she asked.

He answered.

She wrote it down.

"Address?"

He gave it, slower, his voice dropping slightly at the end.

She wrote, then checked the box, then moved to the next line.

"Anyone with you?"

He shook his head.

She marked the space and pushed the form forward, her finger landing on the line before lifting again. He signed, then stepped aside, his hands dropping to his sides as he moved out of the way.

"Next."

The rhythm held.

She shifted her stance again, this time placing more weight on her back foot for a moment before returning forward. The movement was small, contained beneath the table, not enough to interrupt the motion of her hand. The pen continued to move, line after line, form after form.

Across the room, the laptop screen updated as another set of names was entered, the rows sliding upward in steady increments. A volunteer called out for a missing piece of information, then lowered their voice when someone answered from closer by. The flow between table and screen continued without interruption.

"Next," she said again.

Another person stepped forward.

She did not look up.

She did not slow.

The line continued to move.

And she remained at the table.

The line pressed closer to the table as another group came through the doors, the space behind the tape dissolving into a tighter cluster that had to be managed by hand rather than marking. A volunteer at the edge raised both hands briefly, guiding two people back half a step while turning to signal where the next group should stand. Bags were set down, lifted again, shifted from one hand to the other as people adjusted their place without leaving the line. The sound of the room changed slightly, more movement layered over the same low voices.

She pulled another form into place, aligning it with the edge of the table using the side of her wrist before her pen reached it. The tip caught once on a wrinkle in the paper, then smoothed out as she adjusted pressure without looking. To her left, the completed stack had been split again, one portion gone, the remaining pile tapped flat and pushed closer to her elbow. To her right, the blank stack had thinned further, the top page already bent forward, ready.

"Next," she said.

A man stepped forward holding a small envelope, the paper creased and softened at the corners. He placed it on the table, then kept his hand resting on it for a moment as if unsure whether to let it go. She moved it aside with two fingers without opening it, pulling a blank form into position beneath her hand.

"Name?" she asked.

He answered, and she wrote immediately, the letters forming in a continuous line. She shifted to the next field before he finished speaking, catching the end of his name without lifting the pen. The envelope remained where she had set it, half under the edge of another form.

"Address?"

He hesitated, his hand still resting near the envelope, then gave the answer in shorter phrases. She filled the line as the words came, leaving no gap where the hesitation had been.

"Anyone with you?"

He shook his head.

She marked the box and slid the form forward, tapping once near the signature line before pulling her hand back. He signed, lifting the envelope again before stepping aside, his movement slower than the line required. The next person shifted forward before he fully cleared the space.

"Next."

A woman stepped in, one hand gripping the strap of a bag slung across her shoulder, the other resting flat against the table. She leaned forward slightly, her posture angled toward the form before she spoke. The volunteer beside the table reached across and moved a clipboard out of the way to make room.

"Name?" she asked.

The woman answered, her voice tight but steady, and she leaned just enough to hear, her pen already moving. The line behind her compressed again, someone stepping sideways to allow another person to join at the end.

"Address?"

The woman paused, her grip tightening on the table edge before she spoke. She wrote as the words came, pressing slightly harder through the middle of the line, then easing again as she finished.

"Anyone with you?"

The woman nodded once, turning her head slightly toward someone behind her.

She marked the space and added a short note in the margin, the letters tighter, compressed between lines. The second person stepped forward when motioned, stopping just behind the first until the form was ready.

She slid the paper forward and tapped once at the signature line. The woman signed, then stepped aside, pulling the other person with her. The space filled immediately.

"Next."

The word did not change.

A volunteer reached for the bottle of water again, turning it slightly so the label faced outward, then setting it closer to her hand. The condensation ring widened where it had been moved. She did not look at it.

"You've been here too long," the volunteer said, low enough that it stayed at the table.

She did not pause.

"I'm fine," she said.

The pen continued to move, the motion unchanged.

The volunteer watched for a moment longer, then shifted attention to the stack of forms, lifting a portion and carrying it toward the data table without saying anything else.

"Next," she said.

A man stepped forward, his hands empty, his shoulders slightly forward as if bracing himself before speaking. He looked at the form, then at her hand, then back to the form again as if trying to follow the motion.

"Name?" she asked.

He answered.

She wrote it down, the pen moving in the same steady rhythm.

"Address?"

He gave it, his voice slowing near the end.

She wrote, then checked the box, then moved to the next line.

"Anyone with you?"

He shook his head.

She marked the space and pushed the form forward, her finger landing near the signature line before lifting again. He signed, then stepped aside, his movement slightly delayed as he cleared the table.

"Next."

The line advanced.

She shifted her weight again, this time placing her foot back for a moment before returning forward, her knee bending just enough to release the pressure. The movement stayed below the table edge, not interrupting the motion of her hand. The pen continued to move, line after line, without pause.

Across the room, the laptop screen updated again, rows sliding upward as names were entered, the list expanding at the bottom while disappearing at the top. A volunteer called out for clarification on a spelling, then nodded when it was given, typing quickly before moving on.

"Next," she said again.

Another person stepped forward.

She did not look up.

She did not slow.

The line continued to move.

And she remained at the table.

The line no longer held a clear shape, folding in on itself where the space narrowed and stretching again near the entrance as more people were brought in. A volunteer moved along the side, placing a hand lightly at a shoulder, then another, guiding people into a loose order that held only as long as they stood still. A cart rolled past behind the table, the wheels catching briefly on a seam in the floor before lifting and continuing. Voices rose for a moment as two people spoke at once, then dropped again into the same contained level.

She pulled another form forward, aligning it with the edge of the table by touch rather than sight, her pen already moving before the page had settled flat. The stack of blanks to her right was nearly gone now, the last few sheets fanned slightly where they had been pulled apart too quickly. To her left, the completed forms had been replaced by a thinner stack, already uneven again from being set down without alignment. The motion between the stacks remained continuous.

"Next," she said.

A man stepped forward carrying a plastic bag, the handles stretched thin where he gripped them too tightly. He set it down at his feet, then rested both hands on the table, leaning slightly forward as if to hear more clearly. His fingers tapped once against the surface, then stilled when she began to write.

"Name?" she asked.

He answered, and she wrote immediately, the pen moving in the same steady rhythm. She shifted to the next field before he had finished, catching the end of his name as it came.

"Address?"

He hesitated, his hands tightening briefly on the edge of the table before he spoke. She wrote as the words came, pressing slightly harder through the middle of the line, then easing again as she reached the end.

"Anyone with you?"

He shook his head.

She marked the space and slid the form forward, tapping once at the signature line. He signed, his hand lingering for a moment before lifting, then stepped aside, pulling the bag up with him as the next person moved forward.

"Next."

A volunteer reached across and pulled the last few blank forms closer, placing a new stack beside them without interrupting her movement. The edge of the new stack caught briefly against the old, then slid into place as the volunteer pressed it flat. The transition happened mid-line, her pen continuing without pause.

"You need to switch out," the volunteer said, closer now, their voice low but firm.

She did not look up.

"I'm fine," she said.

The words came the same as before, without change in tone or pace.

The volunteer stayed a moment longer, watching her hand as it moved, then reached for the completed stack instead, lifting it and carrying it away. Another volunteer stepped into their place, sorting forms without speaking.

"Next," she said.

A woman stepped forward, one hand gripping the strap of a backpack, the other resting lightly on the table. She shifted her weight from one foot to the other as she waited for the question, her gaze fixed on the form in front of her.

"Name?" she asked.

The woman answered, and she wrote it down, the pen moving steadily across the line. The room behind them shifted again as another group entered, the door opening wide before closing, the sound of the hallway carrying in and then fading.

"Address?"

The woman paused, her fingers tightening on the strap before she spoke. She leaned slightly closer, just enough to hear, and filled the line as the words came, not waiting for them to settle.

"Anyone with you?"

The woman nodded once, glancing back over her shoulder.

She marked the space and added a short note in the margin, the letters compressed between lines. A second person stepped forward when motioned, stopping just behind her shoulder.

She slid the form forward and tapped once at the signature line. The woman signed, then stepped aside, pulling the other person with her as the line shifted again.

"Next."

The word held.

She shifted her stance again, this time placing more weight onto her back foot, her knee bending slightly before she straightened again. The movement was small but slower than before, her balance adjusting before settling. Her pen did not stop.

A phone rang behind her, louder than the others, then cut off as it was answered. A voice rose briefly, then dropped again, the conversation contained.

"Next," she said.

A man stepped forward, then stopped, his hands hovering near the table before settling on the edge. He looked at the form, then at her hand, then back again as if trying to follow the motion.

"Name?" she asked.

He answered.

She wrote it down.

"Address?"

He gave it, slower this time.

She wrote, then checked the box, then moved to the next line.

"Anyone with you?"

He shook his head.

She marked the space and pushed the form forward, her finger landing near the line before lifting again. He signed, then stepped aside, his movement delayed as the next person stepped forward too quickly, then corrected.

"Next."

The rhythm continued.

Across the room, the laptop screen updated again, rows shifting upward, the list expanding as names were entered. A volunteer called out for clarification, then nodded when it was given, typing quickly before moving on.

She pulled the next form forward.

Her hand moved.

She did not look up.

She did not step away.

The line continued to move.

And she remained at the table.

The line had thinned slightly near the table, not because fewer people were coming, but because more space had been pushed toward the entrance where volunteers were trying to reorganize the flow. A voice called out for spacing, then repeated it, guiding people back half a step before turning to receive another group entering through the doors. A cart rolled past again, slower this time, the wheels rattling briefly before settling as it cleared the uneven seam in the floor. The room held its shape, but only because it was constantly being adjusted.

She pulled another form forward, but her hand paused a fraction longer than before as the page caught against the edge of the stack. She pressed it flat with the side of her hand, then continued writing, the pen moving but not as quickly as it had earlier. The stack of blanks beside her had been replaced again, the new pages sharper, less worn, but already bending at the corners where they were being pulled forward. To her left, the completed stack had spread wider, no longer holding a clean edge.

"Next," she said.

A man stepped forward, then waited a beat longer than the others before speaking, watching her hand as it moved. His hands rested on the table, then shifted, then stilled again as if he had chosen a position and decided not to move from it.

"Name?" she asked.

He answered.

She wrote it down, the pen dragging slightly at the start of the line before smoothing out. She shifted to the next field, but her hand lifted briefly between lines before returning to the page.

"Address?"

He gave it.

She wrote again, the letters forming slower now, each one placed rather than flowing into the next.

"Anyone with you?"

He shook his head.

She marked the box and slid the form forward, her finger landing near the signature line but not as precisely as before. He signed, then stepped aside, clearing the space more slowly than the line expected.

"Next."

A volunteer stepped closer to the table, not reaching in this time, just standing within the edge of her movement.

"You need to step away," they said.

She did not look up.

"I'm fine," she said.

The words came, but the pen paused again before continuing.

The volunteer did not move immediately.

"You've been here since opening," they said.

She did not respond.

She pulled the next form forward, but the page slid unevenly, catching at the corner before she pressed it flat again. The pen hovered just above the line for a moment before touching down.

"Next," she said.

A woman stepped forward, her hands gripping the edge of the table, her shoulders angled inward. The line behind her shifted again, someone stepping forward too quickly before being pulled back by a volunteer at the side.

"Name?" she asked.

The woman answered.

She wrote it down, the pen moving slower, the letters slightly heavier where she pressed harder than before.

"Address?"

The woman hesitated.

She waited, but her hand did not move until the words came.

She wrote, then paused again before checking the box.

"Anyone with you?"

The woman shook her head.

She marked the space and pushed the form forward, her finger landing near the line but sliding slightly before stopping. The woman signed, then stepped aside.

"Next."

The word came, but not as quickly.

The volunteer remained beside her.

"You're shaking," they said.

She did not look up.

Her hand rested on the table for a moment, the pen still in her grip, before she lifted it again.

"I'm fine," she said.

But her hand did not return to the page immediately.

Across the room, the laptop updated again, rows shifting upward, the list continuing to grow. A volunteer called out for a missing piece of information, then lowered their voice when it was answered. The movement of the room did not stop.

The person at the front of the line did not step forward.

They waited.

She looked down at the form.

The line for the next name was empty.

Her pen hovered above it.

The volunteer reached in, placing a hand lightly on the edge of the table, not touching her, but close enough that the movement registered.

"You need to step away," they said again.

The line held.

The room continued.

She lowered the pen.

Not onto the page.

Onto the table.

The sound was small but distinct.

She did not pick it back up.

For a moment, nothing moved at the table.

Then the volunteer stepped forward into the space she had occupied, pulling the form into place, picking up a pen from the stack, aligning the page with the edge.

"Next," the volunteer said.

The line moved.

She remained where she was for a second longer, her hands now empty, her weight still forward as if she had not yet shifted out of position.

Then she stepped back.

One step.

Then another.

The space at the table closed immediately.

The forms continued to move.

The names continued to be written.

The bottle of water remained unopened where it had been set.

And she was no longer at the table.

STORY 7

The National Guard Line

THE LINE RAN ACROSS the street from one curb to the other, marked by a length of plastic barrier tape that had been tied to a signpost on one end and looped around a traffic cone on the other. Two vehicles were parked at angles behind it, blocking the open lane, their engines off but still warm from recent movement. Beyond the tape, the road continued into the neighborhood, the houses visible but partially obscured by a rise in the street and the angle of the block. The air carried the smell of damp wood and something burned beneath it, faint but persistent.

He stood just behind the tape with his feet set shoulder-width apart, his weight balanced evenly, one hand resting near the strap across his chest while the other hung free at his side. The uniform held its shape despite the movement of the day, the fabric creased where it had been worn, the sleeves marked with dust near the cuffs. A radio clipped at his shoulder gave a short burst of static, then went quiet again. The tape shifted slightly in the wind, lifting and settling against the cone.

"Hold the line," the voice had said earlier.

No further instruction had followed.

A man approached from the far side of the street, moving faster than the others had, his steps uneven as he closed the distance. He slowed only when he reached the tape, his hand lifting as if to push it aside before stopping just short. His breathing was visible in the rise of his shoulders, his gaze fixed past the barrier toward the houses beyond.

"I need to get through," the man said.

He did not move.

"You can't go past the line," he said.

The words came without change in tone, the same as he had used before, the same as he would use again.

"My house is right there," the man said, pointing past the tape toward the far end of the block. "It's still standing."

He followed the direction of the gesture briefly, then returned his gaze to the man.

"You can't go past the line," he repeated.

The tape shifted again in the wind, lifting slightly before settling back into place. A second guard stood several feet down the line, mirroring his position, their stance angled slightly toward the center where the pressure was greatest. Behind them, another vehicle adjusted position, its tires turning slightly before stopping again.

The man stepped closer, the toe of his shoe nearly touching the tape.

"I just need five minutes," he said.

He did not step back.

"You can't go past the line."

The man's hand lifted again, hovering over the tape, then dropping to his side. He shifted his weight from one foot to the other, his stance tightening as he looked past the barrier again.

"There's no one there," the man said. "I checked this morning."

He did not respond immediately.

The radio at his shoulder gave another short burst of static, then cleared. A voice spoke briefly, too low to carry fully, then cut out again. The message did not change his position.

"You need to step back," he said.

The man did not move.

A woman approached from behind, slower, carrying a bag in one hand, her steps measured as she came up beside the man. She stopped just short of the tape, her gaze moving from him to the guard and back again.

"They're not letting anyone through," she said.

The man did not look at her.

"I just need to check," he said.

The tape lifted again in the wind, brushing lightly against the man's leg before falling back. He shifted his stance slightly, placing more weight onto his back foot without stepping away from the line.

"You need to step back," he said again.

The woman placed her hand lightly on the man's arm, not pulling, just resting it there.

"They said to wait," she said.

The man shook his head once, his eyes still fixed past the barrier.

"They don't know," he said.

He remained where he was, his posture unchanged, his position fixed relative to the tape. The street behind the man filled gradually as more people approached, stopping at varying distances, forming a loose line that did not hold its shape for long. A volunteer moved along the edge, speaking quietly, guiding people to stand back, then stepping away as the space shifted again.

"You need to step back," he said.

The man exhaled, the movement visible in the drop of his shoulders, but did not move away. His hand lifted once more, this time brushing lightly against the tape before falling again.

"I can see it from here," the man said.

He did not respond.

The second guard down the line shifted slightly, adjusting their stance as another person approached further along the barrier. The tape tightened briefly where it had been pulled, then slackened again.

"Step back," he said.

The man remained.

The woman's hand stayed on his arm.

The line held.

And the space beyond it remained closed.

The line thickened as more people gathered along the tape, the space between them tightening where the street narrowed and opening again where volunteers tried to hold a gap. A second cluster formed ten yards down, voices rising there before settling as another guard stepped forward and repeated the same instruction. A truck idled briefly behind the barrier, then shut off, the ticking of the engine audible as it cooled. The tape stretched slightly between the cone and the post, pulled by small, repeated touches.

He shifted his stance by half a step to keep the center of the pressure in front of him, aligning his shoulders with the man and the space just beyond the tape. The radio at his shoulder gave a short burst, then a voice came through more clearly.

"Maintain position. No entry," it said.

He pressed the button once in acknowledgment, then released it without speaking further. The instruction did not change his posture.

"Step back," he said.

The man did not move.

A second man approached from the side, moving faster than the others, stopping just short of the tape and turning his body to angle between them. He pointed down the street, his hand cutting through the air toward a house partially visible beyond the rise.

"My parents are there," he said. "They don't have a car."

He kept his gaze forward.

"You can't go past the line," he said.

The second man stepped closer, his foot crossing the blue tape on the ground but stopping at the barrier tape itself. The plastic lifted slightly as his knee brushed it, then settled back against the cone.

"They need help," he said.

The woman beside the first man tightened her grip slightly, her hand shifting from his arm to his sleeve, then back again. The first man leaned forward a fraction, his weight moving toward the tape without crossing it.

"You can't go past the line," he said again.

A volunteer moved in from the side, stepping between two people further down, speaking quietly while guiding them back a step. The movement did not reach the center where the two men stood. The pressure held there.

"Who's checking those houses?" the second man asked.

He did not answer.

The radio crackled again, another voice overlapping briefly before clearing.

"Teams are working the area," the transmission said. "No civilians past the barrier."

He lowered his hand from the radio and returned it to his side.

"You can't go past the line."

The second man exhaled sharply, his shoulders lifting and dropping once before settling. He shifted his weight forward again, his foot pressing against the edge of the tape.

"They told us to leave," he said. "Now you're telling us we can't go back."

The first man nodded once, not looking away from the houses beyond.

"They don't know what's there," he added.

He adjusted his stance again, placing more weight onto his back foot, then returning forward, keeping his position fixed relative to the tape. The barrier lifted slightly again as it caught the movement of air, then settled.

"You need to step back," he said.

Neither man moved.

A third person approached, slower, stopping a few feet behind them, listening without speaking. The group behind them shifted again, forming a tighter arc around the center of the line. A voice rose briefly from further down, then dropped as another guard stepped into that space.

The second man reached toward the tape, his hand closing around it for a moment before releasing it. The plastic twisted slightly, then snapped back into place.

"I'm going through," he said.

He stepped forward.

The movement was small, but enough.

He stepped into it.

Closing the distance between himself and the tape, placing his body directly in the path, his hand lifting slightly, not touching the man but occupying the space he would need to cross.

"You're not going past the line," he said.

The second man stopped.

For a moment, neither moved.

The first man shifted closer, his shoulder nearly touching the second, the two of them aligned at the front of the pressure. The woman stepped back half a step, her hand dropping from the sleeve as the space tightened.

"You're going to stop us?" the second man asked.

He did not answer.

He held his position.

The tape stretched between them, a narrow strip marking the boundary neither had crossed.

The radio remained quiet.

The vehicles behind him did not move.

"Step back," he said.

The second man did not.

The first man did not.

The line held.

And the space between them did not open.

The space at the center of the line tightened further as more people pressed in behind the two men, the loose arc becoming a denser cluster that pushed forward in small, uneven shifts. A volunteer moved along the edge, placing a hand lightly against a shoulder, then another, guiding people back half a step before turning to address someone further down. The adjustment held for a moment, then softened again as others filled the gap. The tape lifted and fell in short movements where it was brushed, never fully still.

He kept his position fixed, feet planted, shoulders squared to the two men in front of him, his hand hovering near his chest strap without touching it. The second guard down the line stepped closer to center, reducing the distance between them, their stance mirroring his without crossing into the same space. Behind them, one of the vehicles shifted slightly, a door opening and closing with a short, solid sound before settling again.

"Step back," he said.

The words came the same, unchanged.

The second man exhaled sharply, his jaw tightening as he shifted his weight forward again, his foot pressing against the base of the cone. The tape stretched tighter between the post and the cone, the plastic line lifting as the tension increased.

"You can't hold us here," the man said.

He did not respond.

The first man leaned forward as well, his shoulder brushing lightly against the tape before pulling back, the movement small but repeated. His gaze stayed fixed past the barrier, tracking something beyond the rise that could not be fully seen from where he stood.

"There's nothing there stopping us," the first man said.

He held his position.

"You can't go past the line."

The radio at his shoulder crackled again, a voice cutting through more clearly this time.

"Maintain the perimeter. No exceptions," it said.

He pressed the button once, then released it.

The instruction did not change anything in front of him.

The second man shifted again, this time placing both feet closer to the tape, reducing the space between them to less than a step. His hands lifted slightly, then dropped again, the motion restrained but visible.

"You're standing in the street," the man said. "That's all this is."

He did not answer.

He adjusted his stance by a fraction, angling his body slightly to keep the space in front of him covered, his weight balanced so he could move if needed without stepping forward.

"Step back," he said.

The first man shook his head once, his breathing visible in the rise and fall of his chest. The woman behind him stepped back another half step, her hand no longer on his arm, her position shifting out of the center as the pressure increased.

"They told us to leave," the first man said again. "Now you're telling us to stay out."

The second man nodded once, not looking away from the guard.

"You don't know what's in there," he added.

He kept his gaze forward.

Neither did they.

A voice rose from further down the line, sharper this time, followed by another voice responding, then both lowering again as a guard stepped into that space. The movement did not break the pressure at the center.

The second man reached toward the tape again, this time lifting it slightly with his hand, the plastic stretching upward between his fingers. The cone shifted a fraction, its base scraping lightly against the pavement.

"Don't," he said.

The word came sharper than before, not louder, but different.

The man paused, the tape still lifted in his hand.

For a moment, the space held.

The first man leaned forward again, his shoulder nearly touching the second, the two of them aligned at the barrier. The cluster behind them pressed closer, reducing the space further, the line no longer a line but a compressed front.

"You going to stop us?" the second man asked again.

He did not answer.

He stepped forward half a step.

Not crossing the tape.

But closing the gap.

His presence filling the space where the man would need to move.

The second guard mirrored the motionfrom the side, stepping closer to the center without breaking alignment.

The tape dropped back into place.

The man's hand released it.

No one crossed.

The radio remained quiet.

The vehicles behind him stayed still.

"Step back," he said.

The words returned to their original shape.

The men did not move.

The crowd did not disperse.

The line held.

And the space beyond it remained closed.

The pressure at the center did not break, but it shifted, spreading outward along the tape as more people stepped closer and then held, the front no longer a single point but a wider band that moved in small, uneven pulses. A volunteer worked along the edge, guiding two people back, then turning to address another group forming near the curb. A door on one of the vehicles opened again, then closed with a heavier sound, the movement drawing a brief glance before attention returned to the line. The tape lifted and settled, never fully still.

He held his position, feet set, shoulders squared, his body aligned with the space directly in front of him. The second guard stood closer now, reducing the gap between them so that the center held tighter. The radio at his shoulder remained quiet for the moment, the earlier instruction still in place without being repeated.

"Step back," he said.

The second man did not.

He shifted his weight forward again, the toe of his boot pressing against the base of the cone, pushing it a fraction before it settled back. His hands lifted once more, then dropped, the motion restrained but ready.

"You're not letting anyone through," the man said.

He did not answer.

"You can't hold all of us here," the man added.

The first man nodded, his gaze still fixed past the barrier, his breathing steady but visible. He leaned forward again, then pulled back, the movement repeating in shorter increments.

"There's nothing stopping us," the first man said.

He remained where he was.

"You can't go past the line."

A voice rose again from further down, sharper this time, followed by another voice answering, then both lowering as a guard stepped into that space. The movement drew a brief shift in the crowd, a ripple that moved outward and then settled again at the center.

The second man reached toward the tape again, not lifting it this time, but pressing it down slightly with the back of his hand, testing the give. The plastic stretched, then returned, the cone shifting just enough to scrape against the pavement.

"Don't," he said.

The word came the same as before—short, controlled.

The man's hand remained there for a moment longer, then lifted.

The tape snapped lightly back into place.

A third guard moved closer from the far side, stepping into position several feet down from the center, closing the line further. Their stance matched the others, angled toward the pressure without stepping into it.

"Maintain the perimeter," the radio said again, the voice clearer this time. "No one crosses."

He pressed the button once, then released it.

The instruction held.

The second man exhaled sharply, his shoulders rising and dropping once before settling. He took a half step back, then stopped, his weight still angled forward, not fully yielding the space.

The first man did not move.

The woman behind them shifted further back, her position now outside the immediate pressure, her hands at her sides, her gaze moving between the men and the guards.

"You're just standing there," the second man said.

He did not respond.

He adjusted his stance again, a small shift of weight, his feet remaining planted, his body still aligned with the space in front of him.

"Step back," he said.

The words returned to their original tone.

The second man looked at him, then past him, then back again, his jaw tightening as he held his position.

"You're not going to move," the man said.

He did not answer.

He did not need to.

The tape stretched between them, the narrow line marking the boundary that had not been crossed.

The vehicles behind him remained still.

The crowd held.

The volunteers continued to move along the edges, guiding, adjusting, holding the shape as best they could.

"Step back," he said again.

The men did not.

But they did not move forward either.

The pressure remained.

The line held.

And the space beyond it stayed closed.

The pressure at the center did not increase further, but it did not release either, holding in place as the crowd settled into a tighter, quieter front. The movement shifted to the edges where volunteers continued to guide people back and then forward again as space allowed, the line reshaping itself without breaking. A vehicle behind the barrier idled briefly, then shut off, the engine ticking as it cooled. The tape hung between the post and the cone, lifting slightly in the wind, then settling again.

He remained where he was, feet planted, shoulders squared, his body aligned with the space directly in front of him. The second guard held position to his right, the third further down the line, closing the gap so there was no opening between them. The radio at his shoulder remained quiet, the earlier instruction still in place without being repeated.

"Step back," he said.

The second man did not move forward.

But he did not move back either.

The first man shifted his weight again, the forward lean less pronounced now, his shoulders lowering slightly as his breathing steadied. His gaze remained fixed past the barrier, but the movement toward it had stopped.

"You're not letting anyone through," the second man said.

He did not answer.

The tape lifted once more, brushing lightly against the man's leg, then fell back into place. The cone shifted a fraction as someone behind him stepped closer, then steadied as the pressure redistributed.

The first man exhaled, the movement visible in the drop of his shoulders. His hands, which had hovered near the tape, lowered to his sides. He did not step back.

But he did not reach forward again.

The second man looked at him, then at the guard, then back again, his stance loosening slightly as his weight settled evenly on both feet. The tension in his hands eased, the fingers no longer lifting toward the tape.

"You're not going to move," he said.

He did not respond.

He held his position.

The radio crackled once more.

"Perimeter holds," the voice said. "Maintain."

He pressed the button once, then released it.

The instruction did not change anything in front of him.

The second man stepped back half a step.

It was small.

But it changed the space.

The first man followed, not fully, but enough that the tape no longer brushed against his clothing. The woman behind them moved closer again, her hand returning briefly to the man's sleeve before dropping.

The line shifted.

The pressure eased.

Not gone.

But different.

A volunteer stepped into the space that opened, guiding two people back another step, then turning to address someone further down the line. The movement spread outward, the cluster loosening slightly, the front no longer pressing as tightly against the barrier.

He did not move.

He did not step forward.

He did not step back.

He remained aligned with the tape, his position unchanged.

"Step back," he said.

The words returned to their original tone.

This time, the second man took another step back.

The first man followed.

The space between them and the tape widened.

The cone settled fully back into place.

The tape hung without tension.

The line held.

The guards remained.

The vehicles stayed still.

The houses beyond the rise remained visible but unchanged, the street leading toward them still empty.

He kept his position.

The radio remained quiet.

The crowd shifted further back in small adjustments, the pressure continuing to ease as the front opened by inches rather than feet.

No one crossed.

No one moved past the tape.

The line remained where it had been set.

And the space beyond it stayed closed.

STORY 8

The Case Manager's Numbers

THE FOLDING TABLES WERE arranged in rows across the conference room, each one holding a laptop, a stack of files, and a printed list clipped at the corner with colored tabs marking different sections. Power cords ran along the floor in taped lines, crossing under chairs and disappearing into wall outlets where extension strips blinked with small indicator lights. A whiteboard at the front of the room held columns of numbers written in marker, some circled, others crossed out and rewritten, the edges smudged where hands had brushed against them. The air carried the low hum of typing, punctuated by the occasional murmur of voices kept close to the table.

She sat near the middle row, her chair pulled slightly forward so her knees touched the underside of the table, her laptop open in front of her with a spreadsheet filling the screen. Columns stretched across it—name, location, damage category, eligibility, amount—each cell holding an entry or left blank where information had not yet been entered. Her hand rested on the trackpad, scrolling the list in small increments while her other hand held a pen over a printed file, marking notes in the margins where something needed to be checked. The movement between screen and paper was continuous.

"Next file?" the person beside her asked.

She slid the top folder from the stack at her right toward the center, aligning it with the edge of the table before opening it. The pages inside shifted slightly, held together by a clip that had been bent and straightened more than once. A photograph slipped forward as she opened it, then was pushed back into place with the side of her hand without being fully removed.

"Case 214," she said.

The number was entered into the system by the person beside her, their fingers moving quickly across the keyboard before stopping as the file loaded.

She read the first page without lifting it, her eyes moving line by line while her pen hovered above the margin, then dropped to underline a section before lifting again. The cursor on her screen blinked in an empty field, waiting.

"Primary residence," she said.

The box was checked.

"Damage category—major," she added.

The entry was selected from a drop-down menu, the cell filling with a color that matched the category. The spreadsheet shifted slightly as the row updated.

She turned the page, her fingers catching briefly on the edge before smoothing it flat.

"Insurance?"

"Pending," the person beside her said, reading from the screen.

She marked the margin with a short note, the pen pressing slightly harder at the start before easing as it moved across the page.

"Leave it open," she said.

The cursor moved to the next field.

The room continued around them—keys tapping, chairs shifting, a voice at the front calling out a number before repeating it more slowly. Someone stood to adjust the whiteboard, erasing a column and rewriting it with smaller figures that fit more tightly into the space.

She flipped to the next page in the file, the paper sliding against the table with a soft sound.

"Household size—three," she said.

The number was entered.

"Any dependents flagged?"

The person beside her checked the screen, then shook their head.

"No flags."

She paused for a fraction of a second, her pen resting just above the margin before moving again to mark the line.

"Okay," she said.

The word was quiet, more a transition than a conclusion.

She looked back at the screen, her hand moving to the trackpad to scroll slightly, then stopping as the next section came into view.

"Estimated loss?" she asked.

The person beside her read the figure.

She wrote it in the margin, then entered it into the field, the numbers appearing in the cell before being formatted automatically into the column.

The spreadsheet adjusted again, the row shifting as totals recalculated somewhere beyond the visible screen.

She closed the file halfway, not fully, just enough to hold her place, then reached for the next one in the stack. The edges of the folders did not align exactly, some thicker than others, some bent at the corners where they had been handled repeatedly.

"Next file," she said.

The folder slid into place.

She opened it.

The movement repeated.

The numbers continued to fill.

And the list moved forward.

The rows on the spreadsheet shifted as new entries were added, the list extending downward while the top disappeared off-screen, replaced by the next set of cases waiting to be processed. A column near the far right updated in real time, totals recalculating as figures were entered, the numbers adjusting by small increments that were not called out but still tracked. At the front of the room, someone erased a section of the whiteboard and rewrote it, the new figures smaller, compressed to fit within the same space. A chair rolled slightly as someone shifted closer to their table, then stopped.

She pulled the next file forward and opened it, flattening the first page with the side of her hand before reading. The paper had been creased at the corner, the fold catching briefly before she smoothed it down. Her pen hovered above the margin, then dropped to underline a line before lifting again. The cursor on the screen blinked in the first empty field.

"Case 215," she said.

The number was entered.

"Primary residence?"

"Yes," the person beside her said, selecting the box.

She scanned the page again, her eyes moving across the lines without stopping.

"Damage category—minor," she said.

The selection was made, the cell filling with a lighter color than the one before. The row adjusted as the entry changed the total further down the sheet.

She turned the page, her fingers sliding along the edge before lifting it.

"Insurance?"

"Denied," the person beside her said.

She marked the margin, the pen pressing harder for a moment before easing again.

"Okay," she said.

The word came the same as before.

She looked back at the screen.

"Estimated loss?"

The number was read aloud.

She entered it, the digits appearing in the field, then shifting slightly as the system formatted them. The total column updated again, the change small but visible.

She paused a fraction longer than before, her hand still on the track-pad, her eyes moving briefly to the column of totals before returning to the file.

"Household size—one," she said.

The number was entered.

"Any dependents flagged?"

"No."

She marked the margin, then moved to the next section without comment.

The file remained open as she reached for the next page, the papers sliding slightly out of alignment before she pressed them back into place. A photograph slipped forward from between the pages, catching against the edge of the table before she pushed it back without lifting it fully.

"Next section," she said.

The person beside her moved the cursor.

She read.

The pen moved.

The entries filled.

Across the room, a voice called out, "What's the cap on this category?" followed by a pause, then a response given from another table. Someone stood, walked to the whiteboard, and pointed to a number before returning to their seat. The sound of typing continued without interruption.

She closed the file halfway, holding her place, then reached for the next one in the stack. The folders had shifted, the edges no longer aligned, one protruding slightly further than the others where it had been pulled out and returned.

"Next file," she said.

The folder slid into place.

She opened it.

The first page held more handwriting than print, notes added in different ink, some overlapping where space had been limited. She flattened it with her hand, her pen already poised.

"Case 216," she said.

The number was entered.

"Primary residence?"

She scanned, then nodded once.

"Yes."

The box was checked.

She moved to the next line, her pen underlining a section before lifting again.

"Damage category—major," she said.

The selection changed the row color again, darker this time, the total column shifting as the entry was made.

She turned the page.

"Insurance?"

"Unknown," the person beside her said.

She paused.

Only for a moment.

Then wrote it down.

"Leave it open," she said.

The cursor moved on.

The spreadsheet continued to update.

The totals continued to adjust.

She reached for the next field.

The pen moved.

The numbers filled.

And the list kept moving forward.

The totals column updated again, the numbers shifting by small increments that accumulated across the sheet, the sum at the bottom recalculating each time a field was completed. A second screen had been opened on the laptop beside hers, showing a running total broken down by category, each line filling as cases were entered. At the front of the room, a new column had been added to the whiteboard, the heading written quickly, the figures beneath it tighter than the others. A voice called out a number, then corrected it, erasing and rewriting it smaller.

She drew the next file into place, aligning it with the edge of the table before opening it. The top page was thicker than the others, a printed summary sheet clipped over the original intake forms. She slid the clip back slightly to read beneath it, her pen hovering over the margin before dropping to mark a line.

"Case 217," she said.

The number was entered.

"Primary residence?"

She scanned the form, her eyes moving across the lines.

"Yes."

The box was checked.

She shifted to the next section, her pen underlining a figure before lifting again.

"Damage category—destroyed," she said.

The selection changed the row color again, darker than the others, the totals column adjusting immediately as the value increased. The number at the bottom of the screen shifted by a larger amount this time, the change more noticeable.

She turned the page, the paper catching slightly against the clip before sliding free.

"Insurance?"

"None," the person beside her said.

She marked the margin, the pen pressing firmly at the start of the line before easing.

"Estimated loss?" she asked.

The number was read aloud.

She entered it, the digits appearing in the field, then shifting as the system formatted them. The totals column recalculated again, the bottom number increasing, the difference larger than the previous entries.

She paused.

Not at the file.

At the total.

Her hand rested on the trackpad, her eyes moving briefly to the bottom of the column before returning to the page.

"Household size—five," she said.

The number was entered.

"Any dependents flagged?"

The person beside her checked, then nodded.

"Yes—two."

She marked the margin, adding a note beside the line, the letters smaller, compressed to fit the space.

"Okay," she said.

The word came the same.

But she did not move immediately to the next field.

Across the room, a voice said, "We're approaching the cap," followed by another voice asking for clarification. Someone stood and walked to the whiteboard, pointing to the new column before speaking quietly with another volunteer. The marker moved again, adjusting a figure downward.

She looked back at the screen.

The totals column held.

The bottom number remained.

She moved the cursor to the next field.

"Assistance amount?" she asked.

The person beside her hesitated, their hand hovering over the keyboard.

"Based on category," they said. "Maximum applies."

She nodded once.

"Enter maximum," she said.

The number was entered.

The totals column shifted again, the bottom number increasing, then holding.

She wrote the amount in the margin, the pen pressing slightly harder than before.

The file remained open.

She turned the page, the paper sliding against the table with a soft sound.

"Next section," she said.

The cursor moved.

She read.

The pen moved.

The entries filled.

Across the room, another voice said, "We need to slow this down," followed by a pause, then a response that did not carry.

She closed the file halfway, holding her place, then reached for the next one in the stack. The folders had shifted again, one slipping slightly out of alignment, its edge catching against the others.

"Next file," she said.

The folder slid into place.

She opened it.

"Case 218."

The number was entered.

She scanned the page, her pen already poised.

The totals column remained visible at the edge of her screen.

She did not look at it again.

She continued.

The numbers filled.

The list moved forward.

And the total continued to rise.

The totals column no longer shiftedin small increments but in larger, more visible steps as higher-category cases were entered, the number at the bottom recalculating with each submission and holding longer before the next change. A second figure had been written on the whiteboard beneath the first, boxed in, the space between them narrowing as updates were made. Someone stood at the front, marker in hand, then stepped back without writing, looking from the board to the tables before returning to their seat. The room's sound did not rise, but it tightened, the pauses between voices shorter.

She pulled the next file forward and opened it, flattening the first page with the heel of her hand before reading. The paper was thinner, the print lighter, with handwritten notes added in the margins that overlapped the original text. Her pen hovered above the line, then dropped to underline a section before lifting again. The cursor blinked in the first empty field.

"Case 219," she said.

The number was entered.

"Primary residence?"

She scanned.

"Yes."

The box was checked.

She moved to the next line without pause.

"Damage category—major," she said.

The selection was made, the row filling with color, the totals column shifting again as the value was added. The bottom number updated, then held, the difference smaller than the previous case but still visible.

She turned the page.

"Insurance?"

"Partial," the person beside her said.

She marked the margin, the pen pressing briefly harder, then easing.

"Estimated loss?"

The number was read.

She entered it.

The column recalculated.

The bottom figure moved closer to the boxed number on the board.

She paused again.

Only for a fraction.

Her hand remained on the trackpad.

Her eyes moved once toward the whiteboard.

Then back.

"Household size—two," she said.

The number was entered.

"Any dependents flagged?"

"No."

She marked the line.

"Assistance amount?" she asked.

The person beside her hesitated again, this time longer, their fingers resting on the keyboard without moving.

"Adjusted," they said. "Not maximum."

She nodded once.

"Enter adjusted," she said.

The number was typed in.

The totals column shifted again, the increase smaller, the bottom number moving, then holding just below the boxed figure on the board.

Across the room, a voice said, "We're at threshold," followed by another asking, "Do we hold or continue?" The response did not carry fully, but the marker moved again, drawing a line beneath the boxed number.

She wrote the amount in the margin, the pen pressing slightly harder at the start, then easing as it moved across the page.

The file remained open.

She turned to the next section, her fingers sliding along the edge of the paper before lifting it.

"Next section," she said.

The cursor moved.

She read.

The pen moved.

The entries filled.

The totals column remained visible at the edge of her screen.

It did not change.

She closed the file halfway, holding her place, then reached for the next one. The stack had thinned slightly, the folders now uneven, one corner bent where it had been handled repeatedly.

"Next file," she said.

The folder slid into place.

She opened it.

"Case 220."

The number was entered.

She scanned the first page, her pen already poised.

"Primary residence?"

She paused.

Then marked it.

"Yes."

The box was checked.

She moved to the next line.

"Damage category—destroyed," she said.

The selection hovered.

The cursor remained.

The person beside her did not click.

She did not look at them.

She looked at the screen.

Then at the whiteboard.

Then back to the file.

The pen hovered above the margin.

"Continue," she said.

The selection was made.

The row filled.

The totals column updated.

The bottom number crossed the boxed line.

Across the room, the marker stopped moving.

No one spoke.

The number held.

She wrote the category in the margin, the pen pressing firmly, then lifting.

"Insurance?" she asked.

The process continued.

The numbers filled.

The list moved forward.

And the total did not go back.

The number on the whiteboard remained where it had crossed the boxed line, not erased, not adjusted, the marker resting in the tray beneath it. No one stepped forward to change it. The column of totals on her screen held the same value, the cell no longer recalculating with each entry, the system pausing at the threshold it had just passed. Around the room, the movement continued—typing, pages turning, chairs shifting—but the rhythm had changed, the transitions between tasks slower, the pauses longer.

She kept the file open in front of her, the page still flattened beneath her hand, the line she had just marked visible in the margin. The cursor blinked in the next field, waiting. The person beside her did not move their hands from the keyboard, their fingers resting lightly on the keys without pressing.

"Next field," she said.

The words came the same as before.

The cursor moved.

She read.

The pen moved.

The entry filled.

The totals column did not change.

Across the room, a voice said, "We've exceeded allocation," followed by a second voice asking, "Do we stop intake?" The response came quieter, not fully carried, but enough that the person at the whiteboard stepped forward, then stopped, the marker still unused.

She turned the page, the paper catching slightly before sliding free.

"Household size—four," she said.

The number was entered.

"Any dependents flagged?"

"Yes—one."

She marked the margin, the pen pressing slightly harder, then easing again.

"Assistance amount?" she asked.

The person beside her did not answer immediately.

They looked at the screen.

Then at the whiteboard.

Then back again.

"Pending," they said.

She nodded once.

"Leave it open," she said.

The cursor moved on.

The file remained open.

She wrote "pending" in the margin, the letters smaller than the others, compressed into the space between lines.

Across the room, someone closed a laptop halfway, then reopened it, the screen brightening again. Another person stood, walked to the front, then stopped short of the board, turning back without writing anything. The marker remained in place.

She looked at the totals column again.

It had not moved.

She did not scroll.

She did not adjust the entry.

She moved to the next section.

"Next section," she said.

The cursor shifted.

She read.

The pen moved.

The entries filled.

The file remained incomplete.

She closed it halfway, holding her place, then reached for the next one in the stack. The folders had thinned, the remaining ones spaced further apart, their edges no longer touching.

"Next file," she said.

The folder slid into place.

She opened it.

"Case 221."

The number was entered.

She scanned the first page, her pen poised above the margin.

"Primary residence?"

She marked it.

"Yes."

The box was checked.

She moved to the next line.

"Damage category—major," she said.

The selection was made.

The row filled.

The totals column did not change.

She turned the page.

"Insurance?"

"None."

She wrote it down.

"Estimated loss?"

The number was read.

She entered it.

The system accepted it.

The total remained.

She paused.

Not at the screen.

At the margin.

Her pen hovered above the line where the assistance amount would be written.

The cursor blinked in the field.

No number appeared.

"Assistance amount?" she asked.

The person beside her did not answer.

They did not move.

She lowered the pen.

Not onto the number.

Onto the margin.

Writing nothing.

The line remained blank.

She closed the file halfway.

"Next file," she said.
The folder slid forward.
She opened it.
The process continued.
The entries filled.
The amounts did not.
The totals held.
The whiteboard remained unchanged.
And the numbers no longer moved.

What Remains

STORY 9

The Animal Responder

THE TRAILERS WERE LINED up along the edge of the fairgrounds, backed into place with narrow gaps between them where hoses and extension cords ran across the gravel. Temporary fencing had been set up in rectangular sections, creating rows of enclosed spaces filled with carriers, crates, and improvised pens made from whatever materials had been available when they arrived. The ground had turned uneven from repeated foot traffic, patches of mud forming where water had spilled and not drained, then drying at the edges into a rough, cracked surface. The air held a layered smell—wet fur, disinfectant, hay, and something sharper beneath it that lingered even after the cleaning crews moved through.

She stepped between two sections of fencing, her boots pressing into the softer ground before lifting again, leaving shallow impressions that filled slowly with loose gravel. A clipboard rested against her forearm, the top page marked with numbers and short notes written in tight lines where space had been limited. In her other hand, she carried a small scanner, its screen dim until she pressed the button, the light flaring briefly before settling. A dog barked from one of the enclosures to her left, the sound sharp and repeated until another responder stepped in to calm it.

"Unit C," someone called from further down the row.

She lifted her head briefly, then lowered it again to the page, tracing a line with the tip of her pen before moving forward. The fencing shifted slightly as she passed, the metal flexing under the pressure of animals moving inside the enclosures. A volunteer knelt beside a crate ahead, speaking quietly through the bars while sliding a bowl of water into place, the movement slow and deliberate.

She stopped at the first enclosure in her section and checked the number clipped to the gate, then matched it to the entry on her sheet. The pen moved across the line, marking the space with a short stroke before lifting again. Inside, a dog stood near the back of the pen, its body angled away, its head turned just enough to track her movement without stepping closer.

"C-14," she said.

The number was entered into the scanner, the device giving a soft tone as it registered the input. She held it steady for a moment, watching the screen until the entry confirmed, then lowered it again. The dog shifted its weight slightly, one paw lifting and setting down again without changing position.

"Water?" she asked.

The volunteer beside the pen nodded without looking up.

"Filled," they said.

She marked the line, the pen pressing slightly harder at the start before easing as it moved across the page. The clipboard shifted against her arm as she adjusted her grip, the corner of the top sheet bending slightly before settling back into place.

"Food?" she asked.

"Done," the volunteer said.

She checked the box, then moved to the next line without pausing. The dog remained where it was, its gaze following her briefly before returning to the far side of the enclosure.

She stepped to the next pen, her boots catching briefly on a hose that ran along the ground before clearing it. The enclosure here held two animals, both lying down, their bodies pressed close together, their heads resting against the side of the pen. One lifted its head as she approached, then lowered it again when she stopped.

"C-15," she said.

The scanner lit again as she entered the number, the screen flickering before settling. The tone sounded, softer this time beneath the noise of the row.

"Water?" she asked.

A different volunteer stood at the far end of the pen, holding a bucket, their hands damp where the water had splashed.

"Just filled," they said.

She marked it, then moved to the next field.

"Food?"

"Half," the volunteer replied.

She paused for a fraction of a second, then wrote it down, adding a short note in the margin. The pen pressed slightly deeper into the paper, the indentation visible even after she lifted it.

"Check again in an hour," she said.

The volunteer nodded once.

She moved on.

The next enclosure was empty, the gate open slightly where it had not been fully latched. A tag hung from the side, the number still attached but the line on her sheet marked with a different notation.

She stopped.

Looked at the tag.

Then at the page.

"C-16," she said.

No animal inside.

She did not call out.

She marked the line, a different symbol this time, the pen moving slower before lifting. The scanner remained in her hand, but she did not raise it.

A responder further down the row closed another gate, the latch clicking into place with a short, solid sound. A dog barked again, then stopped as someone spoke to it, their voice low and steady.

She stepped past the empty pen and moved to the next, her boots shifting the gravel as she adjusted her footing. The enclosure held a cat in a carrier placed near the back, the door partially covered with a towel that had been draped over it to reduce the light.

"C-17," she said.

The scanner lit.

The tone sounded.

She knelt slightly, not fully lowering herself, just enough to see the carrier more clearly. The cat did not move, its body pressed against the back corner, its eyes open but still.

"Water?" she asked.

A volunteer behind her answered.

"Inside the carrier."

She marked it.

"Food?"

"Not yet."

She wrote it down, the pen pressing firmly at the start of the line before easing as it moved across.

"I'll come back," the volunteer said.

She nodded once.

She stood.

Moved to the next enclosure.

The pattern held.

Numbers matched to tags.

Entries marked.

Voices kept low.

The smell remained constant, the disinfectant sharp where it had been applied more recently, fading where it had not reached yet. A hose was dragged across the ground behind her, the movement leaving a wet line that spread slowly into the gravel before settling.

She reached the end of the row and turned, scanning the line of enclosures again, her eyes moving from one to the next, checking for anything that had shifted out of place. A volunteer raised a hand briefly from across the aisle, signaling for attention, then lowered it when another responder stepped toward them.

She looked back at her sheet.

The lines filled.

The boxes checked.

The notes added.

She moved back to the first pen, her steps retracing the path she had just taken, the ground shifting slightly underfoot where it had already been pressed down. The dog in the first enclosure remained at the back, its position unchanged, its gaze lifting briefly as she approached again.

"C-14," she said.

The number was already marked.

She did not write it again.

She looked at the pen.

At the water.

At the animal.

Then back to the page.

Her pen hovered above the next line.

Then moved.

The entries continued.

The numbers held.

And the row remained full.

She moved down the row again, slower this time, not repeating the full check but watching for what had shifted since the first pass. The ground beneath her boots had softened further where water had spilled, the gravel pushing aside to expose darker soil that held the moisture longer. A volunteer carried a stack of empty bowls past her, the plastic edges clicking together with each step before settling as they were set down near the next section. The fencing rattled briefly as something inside one of the pens pressed against it, then stilled.

She stopped at C-14 again, not raising the scanner this time, her attention on the dog rather than the tag. The animal had moved closer to the center of the pen, its stance still angled away but less fixed than before, its head turning as she approached. A bowl of water sat near the gate, the surface disturbed slightly where it had been nudged but still mostly full.

"Still not eating?" she asked.

The volunteer from earlier stood a few feet away, wiping their hands on a towel that had already been used too many times.

"Hasn't touched it," they said.

She nodded once, her eyes moving from the dog to the food bowl, then back again. The pen remained intact, the latch secured, the space contained.

She made a short note on the sheet, pressing the pen harder than before, the line darker, more deliberate. The clipboard shifted against her arm as she adjusted her grip, the edge of the paper catching briefly before settling.

"Check again after next round," she said.

The volunteer nodded.

She moved on.

At C-15, the two animals had separated slightly, one now sitting upright while the other remained lying down, their bodies no longer pressed together. The bowl had been moved closer to the gate, the water level lower than before.

"Food?" she asked.

"Finished," the volunteer said, stepping closer to the pen.

She marked it, the pen moving in a short, controlled line, then added a second note beneath the first, compressing the letters to fit the space.

"Refill," she said.

The volunteer bent to retrieve another bowl, the movement quick, practiced, then set it down inside the pen through the gate opening.

She watched for a moment, just long enough to see one of the animals shift closer, then moved on.

C-16 remained empty.

The gate had been closed now, the latch secured, the tag still hanging from the side but turned slightly so the number was angled away from the row. The ground inside the enclosure showed marks where something had been moved, the surface uneven, disturbed.

She stopped.

Looked at the tag.

Then at her sheet.

The notation remained.

She did not raise the scanner.

A responder passed behind her carrying a carrier, the animal inside shifting slightly as the movement changed its balance. The responder moved quickly, not stopping, heading toward the intake area at the far end of the row.

"Transfer?" she asked, without turning.

"Medical," the responder said, continuing past.

She nodded once.

She marked a second symbol beside the first, the pen moving slower, the line slightly uneven where it pressed into the paper.

Then she stepped forward.

At C-17, the towel had been adjusted, pulled slightly back from the carrier door so that more light reached inside. The cat had shifted position, now closer to the front of the carrier, its body still low, but its head raised.

"Food?" she asked.

The same volunteer stepped up beside her, holding a small dish.

"About to," they said.

She nodded, watching as the dish was slid carefully through the opening, the movement slow enough to avoid startling the animal. The cat did not retreat, but it did not move forward either, its eyes tracking the motion without committing.

She wrote it down.

Added a short note.

"Leave it," she said.

The volunteer withdrew their hand, the carrier door closing again with a soft click.

She stood.

Moved to the next enclosure.

The pattern held, but not evenly.

Some pens showed movement—animals shifting, bowls emptying, water levels dropping—while others remained unchanged, the same position held from one pass to the next. A dog further down barked once, then again, the sound sharper than before until another responder stepped in, speaking quietly, the tone steady until the barking stopped.

She reached the midpoint of the row and paused, not to stop working but to reorient, her eyes moving across the enclosures, tracking what had changed and what had not. A hose had been dragged across the aisle, leaving a darker line that spread slowly into the gravel, the water pooling briefly before disappearing.

"Unit C update?" someone called from the far end.

She lifted the clipboard slightly, flipping the top page back just enough to check the summary at the corner.

"Three flagged," she said.

The numbers were written quickly, the pen moving without hesitation.

"Two stable, one medical."

The voice acknowledged, then moved on to the next unit.

She lowered the page.

Adjusted her grip.

Moved forward again.

At the next enclosure, a dog stood at the gate, pressing its nose briefly against the metal before pulling back. The bowl inside was empty, the water nearly gone.

"Water," she said.

A volunteer stepped in immediately, lifting the bowl and replacing it, the motion practiced, the refill quick.

She marked it.

The pen moved.

The line filled.

She did not look up.

Further down, a responder crouched beside a crate, speaking softly, their hand resting near the opening without entering it. The animal inside shifted, then settled again, the movement small but visible.

She reached the end of the row again and turned, her boots pressing into the same path, the ground more compact now from repeated movement. The enclosures stretched in front of her, each one holding its own pattern, its own level of change.

She looked at the sheet.

At the marks.

At the notes.

Then back at the row.

Her pen hovered.

Then moved again.

The entries continued.

The numbers held.

And the work did not stop.

She moved into the next row, stepping over the low line of a hose that had been dragged across the aisle and left in place, its surface still damp where water continued to run through it. The gravel here had been churned more heavily, the ground softer underfoot where repeated crossings had broken the top layer apart. A stack of carriers sat along the far edge, some empty, some holding animals that shifted when someone passed too close, the movement contained but constant. The air felt thicker in this section, the smell of disinfectant stronger where it had been applied more recently.

She stopped at the first enclosure and checked the number, her pen already poised over the line before her eyes finished scanning the tag. The animal inside—a medium-sized dog—stood near the front of the pen, its body angled toward the gate, its tail low but moving slightly as she approached. A bowl of water sat tipped against the side, the surface partially spilled into the dirt beneath it.

"D-01," she said.

The scanner lit.

The tone sounded.

She knelt just enough to reach the gate latch, not opening it, but adjusting the bowl with the tip of her boot until it settled upright again. The water inside shifted, then steadied.

"Water?" she asked.

A volunteer behind her answered.

"Needs refill."

She marked it, the pen pressing firmly at the start of the line, then easing as it moved across. The dog stepped closer to the gate, then stopped, its nose lowering toward the bowl but not touching it.

"Food?" she asked.

"Not yet."

She wrote it down, adding a short note beside the entry, the letters tighter than the line above.

"Flag it," she said.

The volunteer nodded.

She stood.

Moved to the next enclosure.

The pattern held, but the spacing between volunteers had widened slightly, the gaps more noticeable where there had been continuous coverage before. A responder crossed the aisle carrying a crate, moving quickly toward the intake area, their steps careful but urgent as they navigated the uneven ground. The fencing rattled briefly as an animal pressed against it, then settled again.

At D-02, two animals occupied the same pen, but they no longer rested near each other, one at the front, one at the back, the distance between them held without movement. The bowl inside had been filled, but neither had approached it.

"D-02," she said.

The scanner confirmed.

"Water?" she asked.

"Full," a voice replied from behind her.

"Food?"

"Placed."

She marked both, the pen moving steadily, then paused a fraction longer before adding a second note beneath the line.

"Monitor," she said.

She did not look up to see if it was acknowledged.

She moved on.

Further down, a pen stood open, the gate swung wide, the enclosure empty but still marked. A tag hung from the side, the number partially obscured where it had been bent.

She stopped.

Stepped closer.

Adjusted the tag with her fingers until the number was visible.

"D-03," she said.

No animal inside.

The ground showed marks where something had been moved recently, the dirt still loose, not yet settled.

She did not raise the scanner.

A responder approached from the far side, carrying a folded towel.

"Transfer?" she asked.

"Returned to owner," the responder said.

She nodded once.

Marked the line with a different symbol.

Then moved forward.

At D-04, a cat in a carrier had pushed itself against the front, the towel covering it partially displaced so that one side was exposed to the light. The animal's body remained low, but its head had lifted, its eyes tracking movement in the aisle.

"D-04," she said.

The scanner lit.

The tone sounded.

She reached out and adjusted the towel, pulling it back into place, reducing the opening without fully covering the front. The cat did not retreat, but its body lowered slightly again.

"Water?" she asked.

"In the carrier."

"Food?"

"Left."

She marked both.

The pen moved.

The line filled.

She stepped back.

The carrier remained still.

The pattern continued, but not evenly.

Some enclosures showed improvement—animals moving, eating, approaching water—while others held in place, unchanged across multiple passes. The differences began to stand out more clearly, the variation no longer blending into the general movement of the row.

She reached the midpoint again and paused, her eyes moving across the pens, tracking the ones she had marked earlier. The flagged entries remained, the notes unchanged, the conditions holding where they had not improved.

"Any updates on flagged?" she asked.

A volunteer further down shook their head.

"No change."

She nodded.

Looked back at her sheet.

The marks held.

She flipped the page, revealing the next set of entries, the top lines already filled from earlier passes, the lower ones waiting.

She moved forward.

At D-07, a dog lay on its side, not rising when she approached, its breathing visible but slow, its body still against the ground. The water bowl sat untouched, the surface unbroken.

"D-07," she said.

The scanner confirmed.

She crouched lower this time, bringing her line of sight closer without entering the pen, her hand resting lightly against the gate without opening it.

"Water?" she asked.

"Full," the volunteer said.

"Food?"

"Placed."

She did not write immediately.

Her pen hovered above the line.

Then moved.

A longer note this time.

The letters pressed deeper into the page.

"Check again," she said.

But her voice did not carry beyond the pen.

She stood.

Moved on.

The row extended ahead of her, each enclosure holding its own condition, its own level of response.

She continued.

The entries filled.

The notes accumulated.

The flagged lines increased.

And the pattern began to separate into those that changed.

And those that did not.

The next section of the row was more crowded, the spacing between enclosures tighter where additional pens had been added after intake exceeded the original layout. The fencing bowed slightly in places where it had been extended and reattached, the lines no longer straight but held in place by extra clips and ties. A stack of folded crates leaned against the far wall, some partially assembled, others still flat, waiting for space that had not yet been cleared. The aisle narrowed as equipment accumulated along the edges, forcing responders to step carefully between obstacles without breaking movement.

She moved through it without slowing, her path adjusting in small angles to avoid hoses, bowls, and the edges of carriers that had been set down temporarily and not yet moved. The ground shifted underfoot, the gravel displaced more heavily here, the softer areas spreading where water had pooled and not drained. A volunteer passed in the opposite direction carrying a crate, pausing briefly to let her through, then continuing without speaking. The air felt warmer in this section, the circulation reduced by the tighter arrangement.

She stopped at D-08, checking the tag, then the sheet, her pen already poised.

"D-08," she said.

The scanner lit.

The tone sounded.

Inside the pen, a dog stood near the gate, its posture alert but rigid, its head turning quickly toward each movement in the aisle. The water bowl was half full, the food untouched.

"Water?" she asked.

"Half," a voice answered from behind her.

"Food?"

"No change."

She marked both, the pen moving steadily, then added a short note beneath the line, compressing the letters to fit the margin.

"Rotate volunteer," she said.

The voice behind her acknowledged.

She moved on.

At D-09, the enclosure held three animals, two standing, one lying down, the space between them limited by the size of the pen. The bowl had been pushed against the side, partially overturned, the water spreading into the dirt beneath.

"D-09," she said.

The scanner confirmed.

She stepped closer, adjusting the bowl with her boot again, but the space inside the pen prevented it from settling fully upright. The animals shifted as she moved, their positions changing in small increments without fully separating.

"Water?" she asked.

"Refilling now," the volunteer said, stepping forward with a bucket.

She watched the movement briefly, then marked the line.

"Food?"

"Placed."

She wrote it down, then paused a fraction longer than before, her eyes moving between the animals, the limited space, the condition of the pen.

"Flag capacity," she said.

The volunteer nodded, though the pen itself did not change.

She moved on.

Further down, a responder called out, "We're out of medium crates," followed by another voice asking for confirmation. The response came quickly—"Confirmed"—and then quieter discussion followed, not carrying fully across the room. A volunteer lifted one of the folded crates from the stack, turning it once, then setting it back down.

She reached D-10, where the enclosure held a single animal that paced along the front, its movement repetitive, back and forth along the same short stretch. The water bowl had been emptied, the food scattered but not consumed.

"D-10," she said.

The scanner lit.

The tone sounded.

"Water?" she asked.

"Empty."

"Food?"

"Disturbed."

She marked both, the pen pressing harder at the start of the line, then easing.

"Replace water," she said.

The volunteer moved in immediately, lifting the bowl, refilling it, and setting it back down. The animal continued pacing, not stopping to drink.

She wrote a second note.

The letters pressed deeper.

"Monitor behavior."

She moved on.

The noise in the row had shifted, not louder, but more constant, fewer gaps between sounds, more overlapping movement. A dog barked, another responded, then both stopped as responders moved between them, voices low but steady. The fencing rattled in short bursts, then settled again.

She reached D-12, skipping D-11 where another responder was already working inside the pen, their back turned, their focus contained within that space. The enclosure at D-12 held a carrier placed on its side, the door open, the interior empty.

She stopped.

Checked the tag.

Then the sheet.

"D-12," she said.

No animal.

The ground inside the pen showed fresh marks, the surface disturbed, the carrier recently moved.

"Transfer?" she asked.

"Medical overflow," someone answered from further down.

She nodded once.

Marked the line.

A second symbol.

Then moved on.

The flagged entries had increased.

The spacing between them had decreased.

She reached the midpoint again and paused, her eyes moving across the row, tracking the marked pens, the ones that required return, the ones that had not changed across multiple passes. The pattern no longer held evenly across the section, the differences sharper now, the stable ones fewer.

"Unit D update?" the voice called again.

She lifted the clipboard.

"Five flagged," she said.

The numbers were written quickly.

"Two capacity, one medical, two no intake."

The voice acknowledged, then moved on.

She lowered the page.

Looked at the row.

Then back to the sheet.

Her pen hovered.

Then moved.

She continued down the line, her steps steady, her path unchanged, though the space around her had narrowed and the conditions within it had shifted.

The entries filled.

The notes increased.

The flags multiplied.

And the space available did not.

The aisle narrowed further where additional pens had been set in place without clearing the original layout, forcing responders to turn sideways in places to pass between enclosures. A hose ran across the center at low pressure, water spreading unevenly into the gravel and pooling where the ground dipped before sinking in. The stack of unused crates had not changed, though several had been broken down and reassembled into smaller enclosures that filled gaps along the row. The air held steady, heavier now, the disinfectant no longer masking what had settled beneath it.

She moved back toward the midpoint, retracing the same path she had taken twice already, her boots pressing into grooves that had formed from repeated passes. The clipboard shifted slightly against her arm, the top pages filled, the margins crowded with notes that had begun to overlap where space had run out. A volunteer stepped aside to let her pass, then moved immediately back into position, their attention returning to the pen in front of them.

At D-07, the dog remained on its side, its position unchanged, the water bowl still full, the surface unbroken. The volunteer assigned there stood a few feet back, watching without stepping closer, their hands still. Nothing in the enclosure had shifted since the last pass.

"Any change?" she asked.

The volunteer shook their head.

"No."

She looked at the animal.

At the bowl.

At the space inside the pen.

Her pen did not move.

She stood.

At D-08, the dog's posture had lowered further, its head no longer tracking movement in the aisle, its body still but not resting. The food remained untouched, the water level unchanged. The volunteer waited beside the pen, hands at their sides, not entering the space.

"No intake," they said.

She did not write.

She moved on.

At D-09, the three animals still occupied the same enclosure, their positions shifting only enough to avoid direct contact, the available space unchanged. The bowl had been refilled again, but it had tipped once more, the water spreading into the ground beneath it before settling into the dirt.

"Still three," the volunteer said.

She looked at the enclosure.

At the fencing.

At the space that did not increase.

She did not write.

At D-10, the pacing had stopped completely. The animal stood at the back, head lowered, the water bowl full, the surface unbroken. The enclosure held its shape without change, the boundaries fixed.

She did not ask.

She moved.

At D-12, the pen remained empty, the carrier still on its side, the ground inside beginning to settle where it had been disturbed. The tag hung in place, unmoved.

"No return," someone said behind her.

She did not respond.

She reached the midpoint and stopped.

Looked across the row.

Across the enclosures that had not changed.

Across the ones that could not change.

"Any available pens?" she asked.

Silence.

Then:

"No."

The word held.

She looked back at D-07.

The dog had not moved.

The water remained untouched.

The volunteer waited.

She stepped forward.

Closed the distance.

"Move it," she said.

The volunteer hesitated.

"There's nowhere," they said.

She did not look away.

"Move it."

The volunteer stepped forward.

Opened the gate.

Carefully.

Lifted the animal.

The body shifted in their arms but did not resist.

They turned.

Another responder moved immediately, pulling a crate aside, shifting it just enough to create a space that had not existed a moment before. It was smaller than the others. Not empty. But enough.

The volunteer lowered the animal into the enclosure.

The bodies inside shifted.

Adjusted.

Compressed.

The gate closed.

The latch set.

The space held more than it had been built to hold.

She raised the pen.

Marked the line.

A new symbol.

Pressed deeply into the page.

Then lifted.

She did not return to the earlier entries.

She did not adjust the notes.

She moved forward.

The row shifted to accommodate the change, the spacing narrowing, the movement within the enclosures becoming more continuous as animals adjusted to reduced space. The fencing held, the structure unchanged, but the contents pressed closer within it.

She stopped once more.

Turned slightly.

Looked back at the enclosure.

The bodies inside no longer held separation.

They touched now.

Not still.

But unable to move without contact.

She looked at the clipboard.

At the last line she had marked.

Her pen hovered above it.

The indentation from the previous entry had pressed through the page, visible beneath the surface, the paper slightly warped where the pressure had been applied.

She lowered the pen.

Drew the next mark.

The line cut deeper.

The ink settled into the groove already formed.

She lifted the page slightly with her thumb.

The mark showed through to the sheet beneath it.

She let it fall back.

Looked once more at the enclosure.

At the bodies pressed closer than before.

Then turned.

Moved on.

The entries continued.

The spacing did not.

And the work did not stop.

STORY 10

The Team Leader

THE STAGING AREA HAD been set up in a wide gravel lot at the edge of town, marked by a line of vehicles parked in uneven rows, their doors opening and closing in constant motion as equipment was moved in and out. Folding tables had been arranged near the center, covered with maps, radios, and stacks of printed assignments that had already been handled enough to curl at the edges. A portable canopy provided partial shade over the command table, though the sun shifted past it as the day moved on, leaving parts of the surface exposed. The air carried a steady mix of engine exhaust, dust, and the low murmur of voices layered over radio traffic.

He stood at the edge of the command table, one hand resting near the corner of a map that had been weighted down with a radio to keep it from lifting in the wind. The map itself had been marked repeatedly, lines drawn and erased, new routes layered over old ones, the surface showing faint impressions where previous markings had pressed into the paper. A grease pencil sat near his hand, its tip worn down from use, the surface of it flattened from repeated contact. Around him, team members moved in and out of the space, pausing long enough to receive direction before stepping away again.

"Team Three is back," someone said from behind him.

He did not turn immediately.

He traced a line on the map with the tip of his finger, following it from the edge of the marked grid toward a section that had been circled twice. The paper shifted slightly under the pressure, then settled again as his hand lifted.

"Where are they?" he asked.

"At the vehicles," the voice replied.

He nodded once, then stepped away from the table, moving across the gravel toward the row of trucks where the team had gathered. The ground shifted underfoot, the loose stones sliding slightly before settling with each step. A door slammed nearby, followed by the metallic click of equipment being secured.

Team Three stood near the back of one of the trucks, their gear partially removed, their posture looser than it had been earlier but not fully at rest. One of them held a helmet at their side, the strap dangling loosely, while another leaned against the tailgate, their hands resting on the edge without gripping it.

"You clear your sector?" he asked.

The team member nearest him nodded.

"Cleared to the line," they said.

He looked from one to the other, his gaze moving across them without lingering on any one person. Dust marked their clothing, the pattern uneven where it had settled into folds and seams.

"Any gaps?" he asked.

The second team member shook their head.

"No gaps."

He nodded once.

"Any contacts?" he asked.

The first team member hesitated, then answered.

"One," they said.

He waited.

"Handled," they added.

He did not ask for detail.

He shifted his stance slightly, his weight moving from one foot to the other before settling again.

"Water," he said.

The word was not a question.

The team moved without hesitation, reaching for bottles, lifting them, drinking in short, controlled motions before lowering them again. One of them wiped their face with the back of their hand, leaving a darker line across the dust.

He watched long enough to confirm the movement, then turned back toward the command table. The map remained where he had left it, the edges lifting slightly now that the wind had shifted direction. A volunteer stepped forward and placed a second radio on the corner, weighing it down again.

"Next assignment?" someone asked as he approached.

He stepped back into position at the table, his hand returning to the map, pressing it flat before lifting the grease pencil. The tip hovered above the surface for a moment before touching down, drawing a new line that extended from the previously marked boundary into an area that had not yet been covered.

"Extend grid to here," he said.

The person beside him leaned in, following the line with their eyes.

"That's outside the last sector," they said.

He nodded.

"Now it isn't."

The grease pencil moved again, reinforcing the line, then lifting.

"Who's up?" he asked.

"Team Two is still out," the person replied. "Team Four just deployed."

He looked at the board beside the table, where team assignments had been written in marker, names and numbers arranged in columns that had been adjusted several times already. One line had been crossed out and rewritten below it, the ink darker where it had been applied more recently.

"Team Three," he said.

The person beside him hesitated.

"They just came in," they said.

He did not look at them.

He looked at the map.

At the new line.

At the space that had not been covered.

"Team Three," he repeated.

The person nodded, turning to relay the instruction.

He stepped away from the table again, moving back toward the trucks where the team was still standing. The movement around him continued—radios crackled, a vehicle started and then shut off again, someone called out a number that was repeated from across the lot.

"Back out," he said as he reached them.

The team member with the helmet looked up.

"We just cleared," they said.

He nodded once.

"Extend the grid," he said.

He pointed, not with the map, but with his hand, indicating the direction beyond their previous boundary.

"Out there."

The team member followed the gesture, their gaze moving past the visible structures toward the area that had not yet been marked.

"That wasn't in the assignment," they said.

"It is now," he said.

The words came without change in tone.

The team stood for a moment longer, then moved, reaching for their gear, securing helmets, lifting packs, the motions practiced and efficient. One of them paused briefly, their hand resting on the tailgate before pushing away from it.

He watched long enough to see them begin, then turned back toward the table.

The map remained.

The lines held.

The space beyond them remained unmarked.

He stepped into position again, his hand returning to the surface, pressing it flat before lifting the grease pencil once more.

"Next," someone said.

He did not look up.

He drew another line.

And the grid expanded.

The map shifted again as the wind moved across the table, lifting one corner before settling under the weight of the radios placed along its edges. The grease pencil lines had begun to overlap in places where earlier boundaries had been extended, the grid no longer clean but layered, each pass leaving a mark that remained even after the next adjustment. A second map had been set beside the first, its surface less marked but already showing new lines drawn in shorter strokes, as if space for longer ones had run out. The table itself held the pressure of constant use, items moved and replaced without being fully reset.

He leaned slightly forward, one hand braced against the table while the other traced the new boundary he had just drawn, following it outward to where the map ended and the blank space beyond had not yet been filled. The edge of the paper curled slightly where it had been handled, the corner bending upward before settling again under his hand. A radio at the far side crackled, a voice coming through briefly before being cut off and replaced by another.

"Team Three en route," the transmission said.

He pressed the button once in acknowledgment, then released it, his attention already returning to the map.

"Time check?" he asked.

"Twenty minutes since last deployment," the person beside him said.

He nodded once.

The number was not written down.

It did not need to be.

He lifted the grease pencil again and marked a small point along the extended line, a reference that connected the new section to the previous grid. The mark was darker than the others, the pressure heavier where the surface had already been worn.

"Next team?" he asked.

"Team Two still out," the person replied. "No contact yet."

He did not look up.

He adjusted his stance slightly, shifting his weight as he scanned the map, his eyes moving across the marked sectors, pausing briefly at the areas that had been cleared, then moving on to the ones that had not.

"How long?" he asked.

"Forty minutes," the answer came.

He nodded.

The time sat between them.

Unchanged.

He did not call them back.

A vehicle pulled into the lot at the far end, its tires crunching over the gravel before stopping, the engine idling for a moment before shutting off. Two responders stepped out, moving quickly toward the table, one carrying a clipboard, the other adjusting a radio clipped to their vest.

"Team Four update," one of them said.

He turned slightly, just enough to face them without leaving the table.

"Go," he said.

"Sector cleared to boundary," they said. "No findings."

He nodded once.

"Any gaps?" he asked.

The responder hesitated.

"Some terrain we couldn't fully access," they said. "Marked on the map."

He stepped aside, allowing them to move closer, their hand pointing to a section of the grid where the line had been drawn but not reinforced. The mark was lighter, less defined, a gap in the otherwise continuous boundary.

He looked at it.

Then at the rest of the grid.

"Fill it," he said.

The responder nodded.

"We'll go back," they said.

He did not confirm.

He turned back to the map.

The grease pencil moved again, reinforcing the gap with a darker line, pressing harder where the original mark had been faint. The surface of the map showed the pressure, the indentation visible even where the color did not fully fill.

"Team Four," he said.

The responder looked at him.

"You're not done," he said.

The words came without emphasis.

The responder nodded again.

They stepped back.

Moved toward the vehicles.

He did not watch them go.

He returned to the map.

"Status board," he said.

The person beside him turned, updating the column where team assignments were listed, marking Team Four as redeployed, the previous entry crossed out with a single line that did not erase what had been written before.

The board held both.

He looked at it briefly.

Then back to the map.

"Next," he said.

The word carried across the table, picked up by someone further down, then repeated again as another responder stepped forward.

"Team One ready," they said.

He looked at them.

Their gear was already secured, their posture set, their stance waiting for direction rather than rest.

He nodded once.

"Here," he said, pointing to a section that bordered the newly extended line.

"Overlap this sector," he added.

The responder followed the gesture, their gaze moving across the map, tracing the line without touching it.

"That's already cleared," they said.

He nodded.

"Do it again."

The responder did not question further.

They turned.

Moved back toward their vehicle.

The engine started.

The sound held for a moment, then shifted as the vehicle pulled out of the line and moved toward the edge of the lot.

He watched only long enough to confirm the movement.

Then turned back.

The map remained.

The lines held.

But the spaces between them had begun to matter more than the lines themselves.

He leaned in again, his hand pressing against the surface, flattening it before lifting the pencil.

"Team Two?" he said.

The radio answered.

"Still working," the voice came.

He listened.

Then pressed the button.

"Report," he said.

There was a pause.

Then:

"Negative contact," the voice said.

He waited.

"Continuing sweep."

He released the button.

Looked at the map.

At the section they occupied.

At the time that had passed.

He did not call them back.

He drew another line.

Extending the grid beyond them.

"Next," he said.

The table shifted as another responder stepped forward.

The assignments continued.

The teams moved.

The map filled.

And the boundary did not hold.

The map surface had begun to dull where the grease pencil had been applied repeatedly, the paper no longer taking clean lines in the same way, the markings layering over one another until the original grid was harder to distinguish. A second sheet had been pulled partially over one edge to extend the working area, taped down at the corners so it would not lift when the wind shifted. The seam between the two pages created a slight ridge that caught the pencil tip if pressure was not adjusted. Radios remained positioned along the edges, their weight keeping the pages from curling.

He stood with both hands near the table now, one bracing the edge, the other holding the pencil just above the surface as he tracked the current assignments. The lines he had drawn earlier were no longer isolated—they connected, overlapped, and crossed, forming a pattern that filled most of the visible area. Only a few sections remained without markings, their edges irregular where the grid had been extended unevenly to accommodate terrain that did not match the map.

"Team Three status?" he asked.

The radio answered quickly.

"Entering extended sector," the voice said.

He pressed the button.

"Report on terrain," he said.

There was a brief delay.

"Uneven. Slower movement," the response came.

He nodded once, though the team could not see it.

"Continue," he said.

He released the button and returned his attention to the map, marking a small notation near their position, a symbol that indicated reduced pace but not a change in assignment. The mark was small, but the pressure behind it was not.

To his left, the status board had been updated again, the columns filling with crossed lines and rewritten entries, the original assignments still faintly visible beneath the newer ones. Someone erased a portion of the board and rewrote it tighter, compressing the spacing so more entries could fit in the same area. The marker left darker strokes where it passed over older lines.

"Team Two?" he asked.

No immediate response.

He waited one beat longer than before, then pressed the button again.

"Team Two, report."

The radio crackled.

Then:

"Still sweeping," the voice came.

He did not ask for detail.

"How far?" he said.

"Approaching edge," the reply came.

He looked at the map.

At the section marked for them.

At the line that defined their boundary.

He pressed the button.

"Extend," he said.

There was a pause.

"That's beyond assigned—" the voice began.

"Extend," he repeated.

The word cut the response short.

A second later:

"Copy."

He released the button.

His hand returned to the map, the pencil marking a new line beyond the previous boundary, connecting it to the extended grid that had already begun to spread outward. The mark crossed into an area that had not been part of the original plan, the surface clean beneath it.

A responder stepped up to the table, holding a clipboard that had been partially filled, the top page marked with notes that had been written quickly and not fully aligned.

"Medical check request," they said.

He looked at the page briefly, his eyes scanning the top lines without taking the clipboard fully.

"Where?" he asked.

They pointed to a location on the map, just inside one of the earlier sectors.

He followed the point with his finger.

Then looked at the rest of the grid.

"Send from current sector," he said.

"They're already deployed," the responder said.

He did not look at them.

He looked at the map.

At the distance.

At the lines already drawn.

"Send them," he said.

The responder hesitated.

Then nodded.

Stepped back.

Moved away.

He did not follow them with his eyes.

The radio crackled again, overlapping voices briefly before settling into a single channel.

"Team One entering overlap," the transmission said.

He pressed the button.

"Confirm full sweep," he said.

"Confirming," the reply came.

He released it.

His hand moved across the map again, tracing the overlapping sectors, the lines now doubling back over previously cleared areas. The pattern had shifted from expansion to reinforcement, the same spaces being covered again while others extended outward at the same time.

"Time check," he said.

"Fifty-five minutes," the answer came.

He nodded.

The number held.

He did not call anyone in.

A vehicle returned to the lot, its tires grinding against the gravel before stopping, the door opening quickly, a responder stepping out with their helmet still on, not removing it as they approached the table.

"Team Five," they said.

He looked at them.

"Go."

"Delayed start," they said. "Equipment issue."

He nodded once.

"Deploy now," he said.

The responder hesitated.

"Where?" they asked.

He pointed.

Not to a clear section.

But to a space between lines.

"Fill that," he said.

The responder followed the gesture, their eyes moving across the overlapping marks, the lack of a defined boundary clear in the way the pencil had crossed itself.

"That's not—" they began.

"Fill it," he said.

The responder stopped.

Then nodded.

Turned.

Moved back toward the vehicle.

He watched only long enough to confirm movement.

Then returned to the map.

The lines no longer defined separate areas.

They defined movement.

He pressed the pencil down again, reinforcing a section where two lines met, the pressure deep enough to leave a groove in the paper.

"Next," he said.

Another responder stepped forward.

The table shifted.

The radios continued.

The vehicles moved in and out.

He did not step away.

"Team Three," the radio said.

He pressed the button.

"Report."

A pause.

Then:

"Nothing found."

He held the button for a moment longer.

Then released it.

His eyes remained on the map.

On the extended grid.

On the lines that had spread beyond their original boundary.

He did not erase them.

He did not reduce them.

He drew another line.

And the grid expanded again.

The map had begun to lose its original structure, the grid no longer a clean set of lines but a layered surface where boundaries overlapped and doubled back on themselves. The seam where the second sheet had been taped down caught the pencil more often now, forcing him to adjust pressure mid-stroke to keep the line continuous. The edges of the paper curled upward between the weights of the radios, the surface rising and falling in shallow waves that shifted with the wind. The markings held, but they no longer separated space as clearly as they had at the start.

He leaned forward again, one hand braced against the table, the other hovering just above the map as he tracked the positions of the teams. The symbols marking their locations had multiplied, some placed over earlier marks, others written in smaller strokes to fit between existing lines. The pattern had grown dense enough that individual paths were harder to follow without tracing them carefully from point to point.

"Team Two status," he said.

The radio answered after a delay.

"Continuing," the voice came.

He pressed the button.

"Condition?" he asked.

There was a pause.

"Fatigue setting in," the reply said.

He did not respond immediately.

His eyes remained on the map.

On the section they occupied.

On the line he had extended beyond them.

"Continue," he said.

He released the button.

The word held.

A responder beside him shifted slightly, adjusting their stance as they updated the status board, crossing out an earlier time entry and rewriting it below in tighter spacing. The column had filled to the bottom, the new entry squeezed into the remaining space.

"Team Three," the radio said.

He pressed the button.

"Report."

"Slower movement," the voice replied. "Terrain worsening."

He looked at the map.

At the section marked for them.

At the line he had drawn into that terrain.

"Continue," he said.

The response came back after a brief pause.

"Copy."

He released the button.

His hand moved again across the map, reinforcing the line that extended into that area, pressing harder where the surface resisted the pencil. The mark deepened, cutting across older lines that had been drawn more lightly.

A vehicle engine started at the far edge of the lot, then stopped again, the sound cutting through the steady background noise before settling back into it. A responder moved quickly past the table, carrying a piece of equipment, their steps uneven where the gravel shifted beneath them.

"Team One status," he said.

"Completing overlap," the radio replied.

"Any findings?" he asked.

"Negative."

He nodded once.

"Continue," he said.

The button clicked as he released it.

The pattern repeated.

He did not change it.

A second responder approached the table, their helmet still on, their face marked with dust that had settled into the lines around their eyes.

"Team Four back," they said.

He turned slightly.

"Clear?" he asked.

"Mostly," they said.

He waited.

"There's a section we couldn't finish," they added.

He looked at them.

Then at the map.

"Where?" he asked.

They pointed.

A small section.

Near the edge of overlapping lines.

He followed the point.

Then marked it.

A short line.

A circle.

A reinforcement of what had already been drawn.

"Go back," he said.

The responder hesitated.

"We just—" they began.

"Go back," he said.

The words did not rise.

They did not need to.

The responder nodded.

Turned.

Moved back toward the vehicles.

He did not watch them go.

He returned to the map.

The lines continued to thicken.

The spaces between them narrowed.

The original grid was no longer visible without tracing it beneath the layers.

"Time check," he said.

"Seventy minutes," the answer came.

He nodded.

The number held.

He did not call any teams in.

He did not reduce the grid.

The radio crackled again.

"Team Two," the voice said.

He pressed the button.

"Report."

There was a longer pause this time.

Then:

"Movement slowed," the reply came. "Request rotation."

He looked at the map.

At their position.

At the distance from the staging area.

At the lines that connected them to the rest of the grid.

He did not move the pencil.

"Continue," he said.

The silence on the other end lasted a fraction longer than before.

Then:

"Copy."

He released the button.

His hand returned to the map.

The pencil touched down again, reinforcing another section where lines had begun to fade beneath newer markings.

A responder at the edge of the table wiped part of the map with their sleeve, clearing a smudge that had blurred two lines together. The underlying marks remained, the surface only partially restored.

"Next," he said.

Another responder stepped forward.

The table shifted.

The assignments continued.

The vehicles moved.

The radios carried the same pattern of calls and responses, the words repeating without variation.

He remained at the table.

The map remained in front of him.

The lines continued to multiply.

The teams continued to move.

The time continued to pass.

And the grid did not contract.

The map no longer held a clean surface, the overlapping lines forming a dense field of markings that obscuredthe original grid beneath them. The second sheet that had been taped along the edge had begun to lift at one corner, the adhesive pulling away just enough that the seam rose slightly above the rest of the surface. Radios still held the pages in place, but the map shifted in shallow movements when the wind pressed across it, the paper rising and settling against the weight. The markings remained, but they no longer separated space in a way that could be followed without effort.

He stood in the same position, his stance unchanged, one hand near the center of the map while the other held the grease pencil just above it. The pencil tip had flattened further from use, its edge no longer sharp, leaving thicker marks that spread slightly when pressed down. The lines on the map no longer defined clear sectors; they overlapped, doubled back, and crossed until they formed a continuous surface rather than distinct boundaries.

"Team Two," the radio said.

He pressed the button.

"Report."

There was a delay.

Longer than before.

Then:

"Request rotation," the voice came.

He looked at the map.

At their position.

At the lines that connected them back to the staging area.

At the distance those lines represented.

His hand did not move.

"Continue," he said.

The response did not come immediately.

Then:

"Copy."

He released the button.

The word held longer than the transmission.

A responder stepped up beside the table, their helmet in hand, their face marked with dust that had settled unevenly across their skin.

"Team Three is slowing," they said.

He did not look at them.

He looked at the map.

At the extended sections.

At the lines that had pushed outward beyond the original boundary.

"They're still moving," he said.

The responder hesitated.

"They're—" they began.

"Still moving," he repeated.

The responder stopped.

Nodded once.

Stepped back.

He did not follow them.

The radio crackled again.

"Team Four," the voice said.

He pressed the button.

"Report."

"Returning to gap," the reply came.

He looked at the section.

The gap had been marked.

Reinforced.

But not removed.

"Fill it," he said.

"Copy."

He released the button.

A second responder approached, holding a clipboard filled with notes written in compressed lines that had begun to overlap.

"Medical check pending," they said.

He glanced once at the page.

Then back to the map.

"From current sector," he said.

"They're already—" the responder began.

"From current sector," he repeated.

The responder stopped.

Nodded.

Moved away.

He did not adjust the assignments.

He did not reduce the grid.

He did not call anyone in.

The radio continued.

The teams remained in the field.

The map remained full.

A gust of wind lifted the edge of the second sheet, the seam rising slightly where the tape had begun to separate. One of the overlapping lines broke at that edge, the mark no longer continuous where it crossed from one sheet to the other.

He looked at it.

At the break.

At the line that no longer connected.

He placed his hand flat against the seam, pressing the pages down. The paper resisted, the ridge still present beneath his palm.

He lifted the pencil.

He did not redraw the broken line.

He did not return to the edge.

He moved to the center of the map.

To a section already marked.

Already cleared.

Already crossed.

The pencil hovered.

Then touched down.

He drew a circle.

Slow.

Deliberate.

Not around an empty space.

Around a space that had already been covered.

The line crossed older markings, cutting through them, the pressure heavier than before. The grease spread where it met earlier strokes, darkening the surface, the circle closing over lines that no longer separated anything.

He did not lift the pencil at the seam.

He pressed through it.

The circle held across both sheets.

Unbroken.

He lifted the pencil.

The groove remained.

Deeper than the others.

He stepped back half a step.

Looked at the map.

At the circle.

At the surrounding lines that now sat beneath it.

The radio crackled.

"Team Two," the voice said.

He pressed the button.

"Redirect," he said.

A pause.

"To where?" the voice asked.

He did not point.

He looked at the circle.

"Here," he said.

The response did not come immediately.

Then:

"Copy."

He released the button.

Another transmission overlapped.

"Team Three," the radio said.

He pressed the button again.

"Redirect," he said.

"To where?" the voice asked.

He did not move the pencil.

"Here."

A longer pause.

Then:

"Copy."

He released the button.

He lowered the pencil to the map.

Not to draw.

To press.

The tip met the paper at the edge of the circle and held there, the pressure increasing until the surface gave slightly beneath it. The layered markings resisted, then compressed, the grease lines beneath blending where they were forced together.

The paper dipped.

The seam split slightly.

A faint tear formed where the two sheets met.

He did not lift the pencil.

He dragged it once across the break.

The line thickened.

Cutting through the older markings.

Through the seam.

Through the place where the map had already begun to separate.

He lifted the pencil.

The groove remained.

The circle no longer revealed what lay beneath it.

It obscured it.

He stepped back.

Looked at the map.

At the surface that no longer showed the original grid beneath the pressure of what had been drawn over it.

The radios continued.

The vehicles moved.

The teams changed direction.

Toward the same ground.

Already covered.

The map remained in place.

The circle held.

And the lines beneath it could no longer be followed.

STORY 11

The Red Cross Worker

The shelter had been set up in a high school gym, the floor covered in rows of cots arranged in straight lines that had begun to drift out of alignment as people moved through them. Blankets were folded at the ends of some, piled loosely on others, the distribution uneven where arrivals had come in waves rather than in a steady flow. Folding chairs lined the walls, some occupied, some holding bags or stacks of clothing that had been set down and not yet moved. The air carried a mix of detergent, sweat, and the faint smell of the meals that had been served earlier, lingering in the space where it had nowhere to dissipate.

She stood near the intake table, a clipboard resting against her forearm, the top sheet filled with names written in different hands, some neat, some compressed into the margins where space had run out. A line had formed in front of her, not straight, but held loosely by the presence of the table, people stepping forward in small increments as others moved away. Behind her, a volunteer sorted through a box of wristbands, separating them by color, then pausing to recount before continuing.

"Next," she said.

The word moved the line forward.

A man stepped up, holding a small bag in one hand, the strap looped tightly around his wrist. His clothing was damp at the edges, the fabric darker where it had not fully dried, the pattern uneven across his sleeves and shoulders.

"Name?" she asked.

He gave it.

She wrote it down, the pen moving quickly across the page, fitting the letters into the space available without lifting between strokes.

"Anyone with you?" she asked.

He shook his head.

"No."

She marked the line, a short notation beside the name, then moved to the next field.

"Medical needs?"

He hesitated.

"Not right now," he said.

She wrote it down.

Handed him a wristband.

"Cot section B," she said.

He took it.

Stepped away.

The line moved.

"Next."

A woman stepped forward, holding the hand of a child who stood slightly behind her, their grip firm but not tight. The child's other hand held a small object, something wrapped in cloth that they did not set down.

"Name?" she asked.

The woman answered.

She wrote it.

"Anyone else?" she asked.

"Just us," the woman said.

She marked two entries on the line, the pen moving in quick strokes, adding a second notation beside the first.

"Medical needs?"

The woman shook her head.

"No."

She looked briefly at the child, then back to the page.

Wrote it down.

"Cot section C," she said.

She handed over two wristbands.

The woman took them.

Moved on.

The child followed, still holding the wrapped object, not letting it shift.

The line moved again.

Behind her, the volunteer dropped a stack of wristbands, the plastic bands scattering across the table and onto the floor. They bent immediately to gather them, moving quickly, their hands sweeping them back into a pile without sorting.

She did not turn.

"Next," she said.

An older man stepped forward, his movements slower, his shoulders slightly forward as if the weight he carried was not in his hands but in his posture. He held nothing, his arms hanging loosely at his sides.

"Name?" she asked.

He gave it.

She wrote it down.

The pen pressed slightly harder at the start of the line, then eased as it moved across.

"Anyone with you?"

He shook his head.

"No."

She marked the line.

"Medical needs?"

He paused.

Then:

"I take medication," he said.

She looked up.

Not at him.

At the space behind him.

At the line that had formed.

Then back to the page.

"What medication?" she asked.

He named it.

She wrote it down.

Added a second notation.

Smaller.

Compressed.

"See medical desk," she said, pointing toward the far side of the gym where another table had been set up, a small line forming there as well.

He nodded.

Took the wristband.

Moved away.

The line closed behind him.

"Next."

A teenager stepped forward, their hands empty, their posture held tight as if unsure where to place them. Their clothing was dry, but wrinkled, the fabric creased where it had been worn too long without adjustment.

"Name?" she asked.

They gave it.

She wrote it down.

"Anyone with you?"

They shook their head.

"No."

She marked the line.

"Medical needs?"

They hesitated.

Then:

"No."

She wrote it.

Handed over a wristband.

"Cot section D," she said.

They took it.

Did not move immediately.

Then stepped aside.

The line continued.

The names filled the page.

The notations accumulated in the margins.

The spacing between entries narrowed as she adjusted her writing to fit more into the same space.

A volunteer behind her finished gathering the wristbands, sorting them again into smaller stacks, then placing them back on the table in uneven piles. A second box was opened, more bands added, the colors repeating.

"Next."

A couple stepped forward together, their movements synchronized, one speaking while the other remained silent, their answers overlapping slightly before settling into a single voice.

She wrote.

Marked.

Assigned.

The pattern held.

People moved through.

Names became entries.

Entries became assignments.

The cots filled in sections that had once been evenly spaced but now held more than they had been arranged to hold.

She did not look back.

She did not track where they went.

She moved to the next line.

"Next."

The word continued to move the line forward.

The gym remained full.

The intake table remained in place.

The clipboard filled.

And the names kept coming.

The line at the intake table no longer held a single shape, bending slightly at the middle where people stepped out and back in, adjusting their position without leaving it entirely. A second volunteer moved to the side with a small stack of forms, directing a few people to fill in information before stepping forward, but the instruction did not hold evenly, some following it, others remaining in place. The gym floor carried the movement in waves, small shifts that passed through the rows of cots as new arrivals moved toward open spaces. The air remained steady, the sound of voices layered but contained within the high ceiling.

She adjusted the clipboard slightly, shifting the top page to reveal the lower lines where space remained, though the margins had already been used to extend earlier entries. The pen rested briefly against the edge of the paper before moving again, the tip catching slightly where previous pressure had indented the surface. A new page had been clipped beneath the first, its lines still clean, waiting.

"Next," she said.

A man stepped forward holding a plastic bag filled with clothing, the contents visible through the surface, damp in places where the fabric had not fully dried. He set the bag on the table, not fully releasing it, his hand still resting on the top.

"Name?" she asked.

He gave it.

She wrote it down.

"Anyone with you?"

He shook his head.

"No."

She marked the line.

"Medical needs?"

He hesitated.

"My wife—" he started, then stopped.

She looked up briefly.

"Is she here?" she asked.

He shook his head again.

"No. We got separated."

She did not write immediately.

Her pen hovered above the page.

"What's her name?" she asked.

He gave it.

She wrote it in the margin beside his entry, the letters smaller, compressed between two lines that had already been filled.

"If she comes through, we'll match it," she said.

He nodded.

His hand tightened slightly on the bag.

She handed him a wristband.

"Cot section B," she said.

He took it.

Moved away.

The bag lifted with him.

The line moved.

"Next."

A woman stepped forward, carrying a child on her hip, the child's head resting against her shoulder, their face turned inward. The woman's other hand held a folded blanket, the edges uneven where it had been gathered quickly.

"Name?" she asked.

The woman answered.

She wrote it.

"Anyone else?" she asked.

The woman shifted the child slightly.

"Just us," she said.

She marked two entries.

The pen moved quickly.

"Medical needs?"

The woman paused.

"He hasn't eaten," she said, nodding toward the child.

She looked at the child.

Then back to the page.

She wrote a note.

Short.

Compressed.

"Meal line," she said, pointing toward the far end of the gym where another table had been set up, a longer line forming there.

The woman nodded.

Adjusted her grip.

Moved on.

The child did not lift their head.

The line shifted forward.

Behind her, the volunteer sorting wristbands had begun to separate them into smaller groups, the colors no longer stacked evenly, some piles taller than others. A second volunteer stepped in, adding more bands from another box, the plastic clicking softly as they were placed on the table.

"Next."

A man stepped forward holding a paper, the edges wrinkled where it had been folded and unfolded repeatedly. He placed it on the table, flattening it with his hand as if to ensure it would be read.

"I was here yesterday," he said.

She did not look at the paper.

"Name?" she asked.

He gave it.

She wrote it down.

"Already registered," he said.

She marked the line.

A second notation.

"Re-entry," she said.

The word did not change her tone.

"Same section?" he asked.

She glanced briefly at the page.

At the earlier entries.

At the margin.

"Yes," she said.

She handed him a wristband.

He picked up the paper.

Left.

The line closed behind him.

"Next."

A young woman stepped forward, her hands empty, her posture held tight as if unsure where to place them. She looked past the table briefly, then back again, her gaze not settling on any one point.

"Name?" she asked.

The woman gave it.

She wrote it down.

"Anyone with you?"

The woman shook her head.

"No."

She marked the line.

"Medical needs?"

The woman hesitated.

Then:

"I don't know where my dad is," she said.

She did not look up immediately.

Her pen hovered.

Then lowered.

"What's his name?" she asked.

The woman answered.

She wrote it beside the entry, the letters smaller, fitting between lines that had already been filled.

"If he comes through, we'll match it," she said.

The words came the same as before.

The woman nodded.

She handed her a wristband.

"Cot section C," she said.

The woman took it.

Moved away.

Her hands still empty.

The line shifted.

The names continued.

The margins filled further, the notes becoming smaller, the spacing tighter as she adjusted to fit more information into the same space. The second page beneath the first began to show through where the pressure of the pen had marked deeper than before.

A voice from across the gym called out for additional blankets, followed by movement near the supply area as volunteers shifted boxes to reach them. The cots in section B filled further, the spacing between them narrowing where additional ones had been added without moving the original rows.

"Next."

An older woman stepped forward, holding a small purse close to her body, her fingers wrapped tightly around the strap. Her shoulders were drawn slightly inward, her posture contained.

"Name?" she asked.

The woman gave it.

She wrote it down.

"Anyone with you?"

"No."

She marked the line.

"Medical needs?"

The woman hesitated.

Then shook her head.

"No."

She wrote it.

Handed over a wristband.

"Cot section D," she said.

The woman took it.

Held it for a moment.

Then moved on.

The line continued.

The table remained.

The clipboard filled.

The entries extended into the margins.

And the names kept coming.

The line no longer paused between people, the gaps closing so that each person stepped forward as soon as the one ahead of them moved away. A second intake table had been set up several feet to the right, but it drew uneven traffic, some moving toward it, others remaining where they had already been standing. The flow across the gym had thickened, the aisles between cots narrowing as more people moved through them carrying bags, blankets, and small items held close. The sound of voices layered more tightly now, fewer pauses between them, the space holding everything without absorbing it.

She shifted the clipboard, sliding the top page back to expose the second sheet beneath it, though the first had not been completed, the remaining lines filled with compressed entries that ran into the margins. The paper beneath showed through where the pen had pressed harder, faint outlines of previous names visible before they were written again. A fresh column had been drawn along the side, extending the space where notes could be added, the line uneven but functional.

"Next," she said.

A man stepped forward carrying a backpack, the straps pulled tight so that the bag sat high against his back, the shape rigid as if packed without room to shift. He did not remove it when he reached the table, his hands resting briefly on the straps before dropping to his sides.

"Name?" she asked.

He gave it.

She wrote it down, fitting it into the narrowed space between two earlier entries.

"Anyone with you?"

He hesitated.

"My brother," he said.

She looked at the line.

"Is he here?" she asked.

The man shook his head.

"He was behind me," he said. "I don't know where he is now."

She did not pause long.

"What's his name?" she asked.

He told her.

She wrote it in the margin beside his entry, the letters smaller, angled to fit between existing notes.

"We'll match it if he comes through," she said.

The words came the same.

He nodded.

She handed him a wristband.

"Cot section C," she said.

He stepped away.

The backpack shifting slightly as he turned.

The line closed.

"Next."

A woman stepped forward with two children, one holding onto her hand, the other walking slightly behind, their movements out of sync as they adjusted to the space. The child in front carried a plastic bag, the contents pressing against the sides, while the one behind held nothing, their hands at their sides.

"Name?" she asked.

The woman answered.

She wrote it.

"Anyone else?" she asked.

"Three," the woman said, nodding toward the children.

She marked three entries, the pen moving quickly, then adding a fourth notation beside them.

"Medical needs?"

The woman paused.

"The little one—" she said, nodding toward the child behind.

"She's been coughing."

She looked at the child.

Then back to the page.

She wrote a short note.

Compressed.

"Medical desk," she said, pointing toward the far side of the gym.

The woman nodded.

Adjusted her grip on the child's hand.

Moved on.

The second child followed, stepping around a cot that had been placed slightly out of line with the others.

The line shifted forward.

Behind her, the wristbands had been separated into smaller stacks, though the colors were no longer evenly distributed, some piles running low while others remained higher. A volunteer reached into a new box, adding more of one color, the plastic snapping softly as they were removed.

"Next."

A middle-aged man stepped forward, holding nothing, his hands empty, his posture still as if waiting for instruction rather than stepping into it. His clothing was dry but marked with dust along the seams.

"Name?" she asked.

He gave it.

She wrote it down.

"Anyone with you?"

"No."

She marked the line.

"Medical needs?"

He hesitated.

Then:

"I lost my phone," he said.

She did not look up.

Her pen hovered.

Then moved.

A short note.

Not in the medical column.

In the margin.

"Lost property," she said.

He nodded.

She handed him a wristband.

"Cot section B," she said.

He took it.

Moved away.

The line closed again.

"Next."

A teenager stepped forward, their clothing damp at the edges, the fabric darker where it had not fully dried. They held a small backpack loosely in one hand, the strap slipping slightly as they adjusted their grip.

"Name?" she asked.

They gave it.

She wrote it.

"Anyone with you?"

They shook their head.

"No."

She marked the line.

"Medical needs?"

They hesitated.

Then:

"My sister was with me," they said.

She did not write immediately.

"What's her name?" she asked.

They told her.

She added it beside their entry, the letters small, pressed between two lines that had already been filled.

"If she comes through, we'll match it," she said.

They nodded.

She handed over a wristband.

"Cot section D," she said.

They took it.

Did not move immediately.

Then stepped aside.

The line advanced.

The names filled the page.

The margins tightened.

The notes began to overlap where space no longer held clean separation between entries. The second page beneath the first now showed through clearly in places, the pressure of the pen marking both sheets at once.

A call came from across the gym for additional water, followed by movement near the supply area as volunteers lifted and carried containers toward the cots. A child began to cry somewhere in the rows, the sound rising briefly before settling as someone moved toward them.

"Next."

An older man stepped forward, holding a photograph in one hand, the edges worn where it had been handled repeatedly. He did not set it down, keeping it raised slightly as if to show it.

"Name?" she asked.

He gave it.

She wrote it down.

"Anyone with you?"

He shook his head.

"No."

She marked the line.

"Medical needs?"

He hesitated.

Then lifted the photograph slightly higher.

"My wife," he said.

She did not look at the image.

"What's her name?" she asked.

He told her.

She wrote it in the margin beside his entry, the letters compressed, fitting into a space that had already been used once before.

"If she comes through, we'll match it," she said.

He nodded.

Lowered the photograph.

She handed him a wristband.

"Cot section C," she said.

He took it.

Moved away.

The line closed again.

The table remained.

The clipboard filled.

The entries pressed closer together.

And the names kept coming.

The intake area had begun to spill beyond the table, the line widening into a loose cluster that extended into the aisle between cots, no longer contained by the edge of the table itself. A second volunteer stepped in beside her, attempting to redirect a portion of the line toward the additional intake station, but the movement remained uneven, some shifting, others holding their place where they had been standing longest. The gym floor carried the pressure outward, the rows of cots adjusting slightly as people moved around them, bags set down and picked up again when space narrowed. The air felt denser now, the sounds overlapping more tightly, fewer breaks between voices.

She flipped the top page fully back, exposing the second sheet beneath it, the first now filled completely, including the margins, the notes pressed into every available space. The new page remained clean for only a moment before the first entry cut across it, the pen moving quickly, the line drawn straight and unbroken. The indentation from the previous page had carried through, faint grooves guiding the pen as it moved across the fresh surface.

"Next," she said.

A man stepped forward, holding a small suitcase by the handle, the wheels trailing behind it, catching slightly on the uneven floor. He did not lift it as he approached, letting it drag to the edge of the table before stopping.

"Name?" she asked.

He gave it.

She wrote it down.

"Anyone with you?"

He shook his head.

"No."

She marked the line.

"Medical needs?"

He hesitated.

"My mother," he said. "She was with me earlier."

She did not look up.

"What's her name?" she asked.

He told her.

She wrote it beside his entry, the letters small but more spaced than before, the new page allowing for a cleaner line.

"If she comes through, we'll match it," she said.

He nodded.

She handed him a wristband.

"Cot section B," she said.

He pulled the suitcase forward.

Moved away.

The line shifted.

"Next."

A woman stepped forward with two children and a third standing slightly behind them, the group moving together but not evenly, the spacing between them shifting as they adjusted to the line. One child held a blanket, the edge dragging slightly along the floor before being lifted again.

"Name?" she asked.

The woman answered.

She wrote it.

"Anyone else?"

"Four," the woman said.

She marked four entries.

The pen moved steadily.

"Medical needs?"

The woman paused.

"The oldest—" she said, nodding toward the child behind.

"He hasn't said anything since we got here."

She looked briefly toward the child.

Then back to the page.

She wrote a note.

Short.

"Medical desk," she said, pointing again toward the far side of the gym.

The woman nodded.

Moved the group forward.

The children followed.

The blanket lifted fully now.

The line closed.

Behind her, the stacks of wristbands had begun to thin unevenly, one color nearly gone while another remained in a higher pile. A volunteer reached for a new box, opening it and adding more to the depleted stack, the plastic snapping softly as it was separated.

"Next."

An older woman stepped forward, holding a purse tightly against her body, her fingers wrapped around the strap so firmly that the knuckles showed pale against the skin. Her posture remained contained, her shoulders drawn inward.

"Name?" she asked.

The woman gave it.

She wrote it down.

"Anyone with you?"

The woman hesitated.

"My husband," she said.

"Is he here?" she asked.

The woman shook her head.

"I don't know."

She wrote the name in the margin, the letters fitting into the space beside the entry without extending beyond it.

"If he comes through, we'll match it," she said.

The woman nodded.

"Medical needs?"

A pause.

Then:

"No."

She wrote it.

Handed over a wristband.

"Cot section D," she said.

The woman took it.

Held it briefly.

Then moved on.

The line advanced.

The entries continued.

The second page began to fill.

The margins still held space, but less of it now, the notes beginning to cluster along the edges.

A voice called from across the gym for additional cots, followed by movement near the storage area as volunteers shifted equipment to create space for more. The rows adjusted again, the alignment breaking further as new cots were placed where openings appeared rather than where structure had originally defined them.

"Next."

A man stepped forward holding nothing, his hands empty, his posture steady but fixed as if he had been standing in line without shifting for some time. His gaze did not settle on the table immediately, moving briefly across the gym before returning.

"Name?" she asked.

He gave it.

She wrote it down.

"Anyone with you?"

"No."

She marked the line.

"Medical needs?"

He hesitated.

Then:

"My daughter," he said.

She did not look up.

"What's her name?" she asked.

He told her.

She wrote it beside his entry, the letters smaller now, the spacing tighter as the page began to fill.

"If she comes through, we'll match it," she said.

He nodded.

She handed him a wristband.

"Cot section C," she said.

He took it.

Moved away.

The line closed again.

The intake table remained.

The second page filled.

The margins tightened.

The notes pressed closer together.

And the number of names that carried a second name beside them continued to increase.

The intake area no longer held a defined edge, the line widening into a clustered front that pressed toward the table without forming a single direction of movement. The second intake station remained active, but the flow between them had blurred, people shifting from one to the other and back again as space opened and closed. The gym floor carried the pressure outward, the rows of cots adjusting in uneven increments, new ones placed where gaps appeared rather than where structure had originally set them. The air held steady, but the sound had thickened, fewer pauses between voices, fewer spaces where silence could settle.

She stood in the same position, the clipboard angled slightly differently now as the second page had begun to fill, the margins already holding compressed notes that extended beyond the lines. The pen moved across the page, the strokes heavier than before, the indentation visible even where the ink had not fully settled. The first sheet beneath it showed through in places, the pressure of earlier entries marking the new page before the next name was written.

"Next," she said.

A man stepped forward, holding a folded piece of paper, the edges worn where it had been opened and closed repeatedly. He placed it on the table, flattening it with both hands before stepping back half a pace.

"Name?" she asked.

He gave it.

She wrote it down.

"Anyone with you?"

He hesitated.

"My wife," he said.

"Is she here?" she asked.

He shook his head.

"I don't know."

She did not pause.

"What's her name?" she asked.

He told her.

She wrote it beside his entry, the letters small, angled to fit between two lines that had already been filled.

"If she comes through, we'll match it," she said.

He nodded.

She handed him a wristband.

"Cot section B," she said.

He took it.

Lifted the paper.

Moved away.

The line shifted.

"Next."

A woman stepped forward with a child, the child holding onto her arm, their grip firm, their body pressed close to her side. The woman's other hand carried a bag that dragged slightly along the floor before she lifted it fully.

"Name?" she asked.

The woman answered.

She wrote it.

"Anyone else?"

"Two," the woman said.

She marked two entries.

The pen moved steadily.

"Medical needs?"

The woman paused.

"He needs his inhaler," she said, nodding toward the child.

She looked at the child.

Then back to the page.

She wrote a note.

Short.

Compressed.

"Medical desk," she said, pointing toward the far side of the gym.

The woman nodded.

Moved on.

The child did not release her arm.

The line advanced.

Behind her, the wristbands had been reduced to uneven stacks, one color nearly gone again while another had been replenished. A volunteer opened another box, adding more, the plastic bands snapping softly as they were separated and placed down.

"Next."

A teenager stepped forward, holding nothing, their hands empty, their posture held tight as if unsure where to place them. Their gaze moved briefly past the table, then returned.

"Name?" she asked.

They gave it.

She wrote it down.

"Anyone with you?"

They hesitated.

"My mom," they said.

She did not look up.

"What's her name?" she asked.

They told her.

She wrote it beside the entry, the letters smaller, pressed into the margin where space had already been used once.

"If she comes through, we'll match it," she said.

They nodded.

She handed them a wristband.

"Cot section D," she said.

They took it.

Moved away.

The line closed.

"Next."

An older man stepped forward, holding a photograph in one hand, the edges worn where it had been handled repeatedly. He did not set it down, keeping it raised slightly as if to show it.

"Name?" she asked.

He gave it.

She wrote it down.

"Anyone with you?"

He shook his head.

"No."

She marked the line.

"Medical needs?"

He hesitated.

Then lifted the photograph slightly higher.

"My wife," he said.

She did not look at the image.

"What's her name?" she asked.

He told her.

She wrote it in the margin, the letters compressed, fitting into a space that had already been used twice.

"If she comes through, we'll match it," she said.

He nodded.

Lowered the photograph.

She handed him a wristband.

"Cot section C," she said.

He took it.

Moved away.

The line advanced.

The second page was nearly full.

The margins held more names than the lines themselves, the entries beginning to overlap where space no longer held clean separation. The pressure of the pen had marked through to the page beneath, the indentations visible even before the next stroke was made.

She shifted the clipboard.

Lifted the top page slightly.

Looked at the space that remained.

Then lowered it again.

"Next," she said.

A woman stepped forward, alone, her hands empty, her posture still but not settled. She did not step fully to the table at first, stopping just short before closing the distance.

"Name?" she asked.

The woman gave it.

She wrote it down.

"Anyone with you?"

The woman hesitated.

"My son," she said.
"Is he here?" she asked.
The woman shook her head.
"I don't know."
She held the pen above the page.
The margin was full.
The line was full.
The space between entries had closed.
There was no clear place to write another name beside it.
"What's his name?" she asked.
The woman told her.
She lowered the pen.
Not to the margin.
Not between lines.
Across the entry itself.
She wrote the second name over the first.
The letters crossing.
Not replacing.
Not erasing.
Layered.
The ink darkened where it overlapped.
She lifted the pen.
Looked at the line.
At the two names occupying the same space.
Then marked the entry.
A single stroke.
Pressed deeper than the others.
She did not adjust it.
She did not rewrite it.
She handed over a wristband.
"Cot section B," she said.
The woman took it.
Held it for a moment.
Then moved on.
She looked back at the page.
At the line where the names had been written over each other.
The letters no longer fully readable.
The entry no longer separate.

She lowered the pen again.
Drew the next line beneath it.
The indentation pressed through both pages.
She lifted the clipboard slightly.
The mark showed through to the sheet below.
She let it fall back.
"Next," she said.
The line moved.
The names continued.
The entries filled.
And the space between them did not return.

STORY 12

The One Who Walked Away

THE EDGE OF THE operation sat just beyond the last marked vehicle, where the gravel lot gave way to a strip of dirt that had been worn down by repeated crossings. A line of temporary fencing had been set up to guide movement back toward the staging area, though it did not extend far enough to close the space completely, leaving a gap where people stepped through when they needed to move between zones. The ground there held fewer tracks than the center of the lot, the surface less disturbed, though the pattern of movement remained visible in overlapping paths that did not follow a single direction. The sound of radios carried faintly from behind, the transmissions less distinct at the edge.

He stood just inside that boundary, his gear still in place, the straps of his pack pulled tight across his shoulders, the weight settled evenly but not recently adjusted. Dust marked the lower edges of his clothing, the fabric darker where it had been exposed to moisture earlier in the day and then dried unevenly. His gloves were tucked into his belt, one edge protruding slightly where it had not been secured fully. He did not move immediately, his posture held as if he had stopped mid-motion and not yet resumed.

A vehicle passed behind him, its tires grinding against the gravel before slowing as it reached the line of parked units. The door opened, then closed again, the sound cutting through the background noise before settling back into it. A responder crossed the space several yards away, carrying equipment toward the center of the operation, their path angled inward rather than toward the edge.

He looked toward the staging area.

Then toward the open ground beyond the fence.

The space outside held no markers, no lines drawn across it, no visible assignments attached to it. The surface remained undisturbed compared to the lot, the dirt holding only faint impressions where someone had stepped through earlier and not returned.

"Team Six," a voice called from behind him.

He did not turn immediately.

The call came again, closer this time.

"Team Six."

He turned.

A responder approached, holding a radio, the strap across their chest pulled tight where it had been adjusted recently.

"They're asking for status," they said.

He nodded once.

Reached for his radio.

Pressed the button.

"Stand by," he said.

He released it.

The responder waited.

"Where are you positioned?" they asked.

He looked back toward the staging area.

At the vehicles.

At the movement that continued without pause.

Then back toward the open ground.

"Edge," he said.

The responder followed his gaze briefly, then looked back at him.

"They're still working your sector," they said.

He nodded.

The words did not change his posture.

"You going back in?" the responder asked.

He did not answer immediately.

His hand remained near the radio.

Then dropped to his side.

"I'll check the perimeter," he said.

The responder hesitated.

"That's not—" they began.

He had already turned.

The movement was not abrupt, but it did not pause.

He stepped toward the gap in the fencing, his boots pressing into the dirt where others had crossed before him, the surface shifting slightly under his weight before settling again. The responder behind him did not follow immediately, their position holding at the edge of the lot.

"Team Six," the radio said again.

He did not raise it.

He stepped through the gap.

The ground changed beneath his feet, the dirt looser, the surface less compacted than the gravel he had left behind. The sound of the operation dropped slightly, not disappearing, but becoming more distant, the voices blending into a single layer rather than distinct calls.

He walked forward.

Not quickly.

Not slowly.

His pace steady.

The straps of his pack remained fixed, the weight shifting slightly with each step but not enough to change his movement.

Behind him, the responder called out again.

"Hey—"

The word did not carry far.

He did not stop.

The open ground extended ahead, the terrain uneven, small rises and dips that had not been leveled or marked. There were no visible indicators of assigned areas, no flags or tape to define boundaries, only the natural contours of the space.

He continued.

The radio at his side crackled.

He did not reach for it.

Another transmission followed.

"Team Six, respond."

The voice came clearer this time, but still behind him.

He walked on.

The sound of his boots against the dirt replaced the gravel he had left, the contact softer, less defined, the impact absorbed rather than echoed. The air shifted slightly as he moved further from the cluster of vehicles, the smell of exhaust fading, replaced by something less distinct.

He did not look back.

The gap in the fence remained visible behind him, but smaller now, the line of vehicles beyond it beginning to compress into a single shape rather than separate forms.

"Team Six," the radio said again.

He did not answer.

He adjusted his path slightly, stepping around a shallow depression in the ground where water had collected earlier and then dried, leaving a darker patch of dirt. His footing remained steady, the movement continuous.

The operation continued behind him.

The calls repeated.

The assignments moved forward.

He walked.

The space ahead remained open.

Unmarked.

Without boundary.

He did not stop.

He did not turn.

The distance between him and the staging area increased, not measured in numbers, but in the way the sound diminished, the voices blending into something less distinct with each step.

The radio crackled again.

He did not reach for it.

He continued forward.

And the line he had crossed did not follow him.

The ground sloped slightly away from the staging area, the uneven surface revealing shallow ridges and depressions that had not been flattened by repeated movement. Small clusters of grass broke through the dirt in places, their edges bent where someone had stepped on them earlier but not fully pressed down. The path he followed did not hold a single direction, shifting in small adjustments to avoid the dips and rises, the line of travel defined only by where he placed his feet. Behind him, the sound of the operation continued, but it no longer carried distinct words.

He walked with the same pace, his stride consistent, the movement of his pack settling into a rhythm that matched his steps. The straps held firm across his shoulders, though one edge had begun to rub slightly against the fabric of his sleeve, the friction visible where the dust had shifted. His hands remained free at his sides, not reaching for anything, not adjusting his gear.

"Team Six, respond," the radio said again.

The voice carried less clearly now, the distance softening the edges of the transmission.

He did not raise it.

He stepped over a narrow groove in the dirt where water had once cut a shallow channel, the edge crumbling slightly under his weight before settling again. The ground beyond it held fewer marks, the surface smoother where it had not been crossed as often. The pattern of footprints behind him remained visible, but the ones ahead were less defined.

He continued forward.

A vehicle engine sounded faintly from behind, then stopped, the noise carried across the open space before dissipating. A second voice came through the radio, overlapping the first, then clearing.

"Team Six, confirm location."

He did not slow.

He did not turn.

His path angled slightly to the left, avoiding a cluster of uneven ground where the dirt had been disturbed more heavily. The adjustment was small, not enough to change direction, but enough to maintain his pace without breaking stride.

The fencing at the edge of the staging area was no longer visible when he looked forward, the space ahead uninterrupted by markers or structures. The terrain opened into a wider field, the surface holding variations in height but no defined boundaries.

He walked.

The radio remained at his side.

Silent between calls.

Then:

"Team Six, report status."

The words came again, less distinct, the signal carrying but not holding its clarity.

He did not respond.

He stepped onto a firmer patch of ground where the dirt had compacted naturally, the contact underfoot more solid for several steps before softening again. The shift did not change his movement.

Behind him, a figure appeared briefly at the edge of the gap in the fence, standing where he had been earlier, their posture fixed as if deciding whether to follow. The figure remained there, not moving into the open space, then stepped back out of view.

He did not look long enough to confirm it.

He continued.

The sound of the operation reduced further, the voices blending into a low, continuous tone that no longer separated into individual calls. The radio carried the transmissions, but they no longer matched what he could hear from the ground.

"Team Six," the radio said.

A pause.

Then:

"Last call."

The words carried, then faded.

He did not reach for it.

His steps remained even.

The ground rose slightly ahead, a gradual incline that lifted the horizon just enough to obscure the lower portion of the staging area behind him. The vehicles, once visible as separate shapes, had begun to compress into a single line at the edge of his vision.

He walked up the incline.

The effort changed slightly, the pull against his legs more noticeable, the pack shifting with the adjustment in angle. The straps held, the weight remaining centered.

At the top, the ground leveled again.

The view ahead extended further, the field continuing without interruption, the surface marked only by natural variations rather than human placement.

He did not stop.

The radio remained silent.

Then:

A faint crackle.

No words.

Then nothing.

He continued forward.

The sound of his steps against the dirt remained steady, the only consistent rhythm in the space around him. The air moved slightly across the open ground, the breeze carrying dust in small, shifting patterns that settled again as he passed.

He did not look back.

The staging area had dropped below the rise, no longer visible from where he stood. The line he had crossed was no longer in view, the gap in the fence no longer marking a boundary behind him.

He walked.

The distance increased.

The radio remained at his side.

Unanswered.

The field ahead remained open.

Unmarked.

And the direction he had taken did not change.

The ground ahead stretched without interruption, the uneven surface forming shallow patterns that shifted with the light rather than with use. The faint tracks that had appeared earlier thinned further, the dirt smoothing out where no repeated crossings had reinforced a path. The air moved more freely here, the breeze carrying across the open space without breaking against structures or vehicles. The sound from behind no longer carried as a continuous layer, only occasional fragments reaching him before fading.

He maintained the same pace, his stride steady, the movement of his pack settling into a quieter rhythm as the ground beneath him absorbed more of the impact. The straps held against his shoulders, though the fabric beneath them showed darker where pressure had been constant. His hands remained at his sides, not reaching for the radio, not adjusting anything.

A small rise appeared ahead, less defined than the one before, the ground lifting gradually before leveling again. He adjusted his path slightly to avoid a section where the dirt had broken into loose fragments, stepping onto firmer ground without pausing. The movement remained continuous.

The radio crackled once.

No voice followed.

He did not look at it.

He stepped across another shallow depression, the edge giving slightly before settling under his weight. The ground beyond held no visible markers, the surface unbroken except for the natural variation in texture.

He continued.

Behind him, the staging area remained out of view, the line of vehicles no longer visible even when he shifted his head slightly. The boundary he had crossed existed only in the distance he had already covered, not in anything he could see.

He walked.

The field widened.

The space between small rises increased, the terrain flattening in broader sections that held fewer interruptions. The horizon remained low, the sky meeting the ground without structures to break the line.

His pace did not change.

The radio remained silent.

Then:

A brief transmission.

Unclear.

Cut off before it formed words.

He did not respond.

He stepped over a narrow strip where the soil had hardened into a thin crust, the surface cracking slightly under his weight before settling again. The sound was softer than gravel, less defined, absorbed by the ground.

He continued forward.

A cluster of low vegetation appeared to his right, sparse and uneven, the leaves coated with dust that dulled their color. He did not turn toward it, his path remaining consistent, the angle unchanged.

The air shifted slightly, the breeze moving across him without resistance, carrying no distinct sound from behind. The operation had receded beyond what could be heard directly, the radio the only remaining connection.

It remained quiet.

He walked.

The incline ahead was barely noticeable, a gradual lift that changed the angle of the horizon just enough to shift what lay beyond it out of view. He moved over it without breaking stride, the effort minimal but present in the shift of his weight.

At the top, the ground leveled again.

The view extended further.

Still unmarked.

Still without boundary.

He did not stop.

The radio crackled once more.

A faint tone.

No words.

Then silence again.

He did not reach for it.

His steps remained even.

The rhythm held.

The space around him remained unchanged.

He did not look back.

The direction he had taken continued forward without deviation, the line of travel defined only by the placement of his feet and the absence of anything that would turn him.

He walked.

The ground remained open.

The field remained unmarked.

And the distance behind him did not close.

The ground flattened into a wider stretch, the variations in height becoming less frequent, the surface smoothing where wind had carried loose dust into the lower areas and settled it evenly. The faint traces of earlier movement had disappeared entirely, no footprints ahead of him, no indication that anyone had crossed this section recently. The horizon widened, the line between ground and sky uninterrupted by structures, vehicles, or markers. The air moved steadily, the breeze constant now, unbroken.

He continued forward at the same pace, his stride unchanged, the motion of his pack settling into a steady shift that matched each step. The straps held against his shoulders, the fabric beneath them darkened where pressure had remained consistent. His hands remained free, his posture upright, his direction fixed.

The radio at his side remained silent.

Then:

A brief crackle.

A tone.

No voice.

He did not reach for it.

He stepped across a section where the dirt had hardened into a thin, continuous surface, the contact underfoot more solid for several steps before returning to softer ground. The change did not alter his movement, only the sound of his steps, which remained muted against the earth.

Behind him, nothing moved into view.

The staging area remained out of sight.

The line he had crossed remained absent.

He walked.

The space ahead remained open.

Unmarked.

A shallow depression stretched across his path, wider than the others, its edges gradual rather than sharp. He adjusted slightly, angling his path to cross where the slope was least pronounced, his movement continuous, the change in direction minimal.

He moved through it.

Up the other side.

The ground leveled again.

The radio crackled.

A voice began.

Cut off.

Replaced by static.

Then nothing.

He did not slow.

He did not turn.

The breeze shifted slightly, carrying dust across the surface in low, uneven patterns that settled again after he passed. The movement left no lasting trace, the ground returning to its previous state almost immediately.

He continued forward.

The horizon remained unchanged.

The field extended without interruption.

The sky held steady above it.

The radio did not sound again.

He walked.

The distance increased.

Not measured.

Not marked.

Only present in the absence of what had been behind him.

He stepped over another shallow ridge, the surface breaking slightly under his weight before settling again, the pattern repeating without variation.

He did not look back.

The direction remained the same.

The line he had taken did not shift.

He moved forward.

The ground held.

The air held.

The space remained.

And nothing ahead required him to stop.

The ground ahead held no change in pattern, the surface continuing in a broad, uninterrupted stretch where the variations in texture came only from wind and time rather than movement. The shallow rises and dips flattened further, the terrain settling into a consistency that did not require adjustment in his path. There were no tracks ahead, no objects placed to define direction, no markers to indicate where one area ended and another began. The horizon remained steady, unbroken, the sky meeting the earth without interruption.

He continued at the same pace, his stride unchanged, the rhythm of his steps absorbed by the ground beneath him. The pack on his shoulders shifted slightly with each movement, the straps holding firm where they crossed his chest, the tension unchanged. His hands remained at his sides, not reaching for the radio, not adjusting the weight he carried.

The radio crackled once.

A faint tone.

Then a voice.

Distant.

"Team Six. . ."

The words did not carry clearly.

They broke.

Faded.

He did not reach for it.

He walked.

The sound did not repeat.

The air moved steadily across the open space, the breeze carrying no distinct direction, no sound that separated itself from the rest. The ground beneath his feet remained consistent, the contact soft, the impact absorbed without echo.

He moved over a slight rise, the incline barely perceptible until it shifted his balance, then leveled again at the top. The view beyond it extended further, the field continuing without interruption, no change in pattern, no indication of boundary.

He did not slow.

He did not turn.

The radio remained silent.

Then:

A final crackle.

A tone that held longer than the others.

No voice followed.

He reached down.

For the first time since he had stepped beyond the fence.

His hand closed around the radio.

He lifted it.

Held it.

The surface showed the marks of use, the edges worn where it had been handled repeatedly, the clip bent slightly where it had been secured and released. The screen flickered faintly, then steadied, the signal indicator dim.

He did not press the button.

He held it in front of him.

Looked at it.

The antenna angled slightly away, not fully straight.

The casing carried dust along its edges.

The tone faded.

The screen dimmed.

He lowered his hand.

Not to his belt.

Not to his shoulder.

He opened his grip.

The radio dropped.

The fall was short.

The ground absorbed the impact.

The casing struck once.

Turned.

Settled into the dirt.

The antenna bent further where it met the surface.

The screen flickered.

Then went dark.

He did not pick it up.

He did not look back at it.

He stepped forward.

His foot passed beside it.

Close enough to shift the dust around it.

Not touching.

He continued.
The radio remained behind him.
Partially embedded where it had settled.
The ground around it undisturbed except for the mark of its fall.
He did not turn.
The field ahead remained open.
Unmarked.
The horizon held.
The direction remained unchanged.
He walked.
The distance increased.
The radio did not sound again.
The object remained where it had fallen.
And the line he had carried no longer moved with him.

Conclusion

What Holds After Everything Gives Way

The operations end in stages, not all at once. Vehicles leave in uneven intervals, some pulling out quickly while others remain longer, their doors open as equipment is sorted and repacked. The maps are taken down last, their surfaces marked over so many times that the original lines are no longer visible beneath what was added later. Tables are folded, radios collected, and the ground where everything stood begins to return to its previous state, though not immediately.

The spaces where the work took place remain marked for a while. The gravel holds impressions where vehicles were parked, the dirt shows where people stood and moved in repeated paths, and the floors of shelters carry the faint outlines of where cots had been placed. These marks do not last, but they do not disappear at once. They fade in layers, the most recent changes going first, the deeper ones holding longer.

The people who worked in these spaces leave them in different ways. Some step away at the end of a shift, returning to vehicles, to rooms, to places where the work is not present in the same form. Others remain longer, finishing tasks that extend beyond the visible operation, their movement slower as the structure around them reduces. A few leave without marking the moment, their departure not announced, their position simply no longer held.

The decisions made during the work do not remain in the same place as the work itself. They are not stored on the maps once the maps are removed, nor do they remain in the tables once those are cleared. They are not visible in the empty spaces where cots or pens or equipment once stood. What remains is not located in a single place that can be returned to and examined.

The objects used during the work carry some of what occurred, but not in a way that can be read directly. A pen may still show the pressure of where it was held too tightly, a page may carry the indentation of a line drawn through it, a radio may hold dust along its edges where it was set down and not picked up again. These marks do not explain what happened, but they do not fully erase it either.

The systems that organized the work remain intact after the operation ends. The structures that directed movement, assigned tasks, and defined roles continue to exist, ready to be used again. They do not retain the specific conditions of any one operation, but they carry the same form into the next one. The work begins again within them, shaped by what is already in place.

The people who return to those systems do so with the same roles available to them. They step back into positions that are already defined, the expectations of those positions unchanged. The work resumes, not from where it left off, but from where the system begins again.

What changes is not always visible at the level of the system. It does not appear in the structure of assignments or the layout of operations. It does not alter the way lines are drawn or how tasks are distributed. The changes are not held in the procedures that guide the work.

They appear instead in smaller ways.

In how long a hand remains on a map before lifting.

In how firmly a line is drawn.

In whether a name is written once or written over another.

In whether a call is made or left unanswered.

In whether a boundary is held or crossed.

In whether something is set down and left where it falls.

These actions do not stop the work. They do not change the system in a way that can be measured from the outside. The operations continue, the structures hold, and the work is done again.

What remains is not a record that can be reviewed or a set of outcomes that can be fully accounted for. It is not contained in a report or captured in a summary. It does not resolve into a single explanation.

What remains is carried forward in the next action.

In the next line drawn.

In the next name written.

In the next decision made at the point where something must be done and cannot be undone.

The work continues.

The systems remain.

The spaces reset.

And what holds after everything gives way is not the structure that contains the work, but the moment in which a person acts within it.

APPENDIX A

Recognizing Moral Injury in the Field

Moral injury in the field does not usually announce itself. It does not arrive as a clear statement or a defined moment. It shows up in small changes—often in the middle of ongoing work—where something shifts but the work continues.

This appendix is not designed to diagnose. It is designed to help you notice.

1. WHAT MORAL INJURY LOOKS LIKE IN REAL TIME

Moral injury often appears while the operation is still active. It is not limited to what happens afterward. It can be seen in the way a person moves through decisions that cannot be fully resolved.

You may notice:

- A responder who completes tasks correctly but slows at specific moments
- A pause that lasts slightly longer than necessary before acting
- Repeated checking of the same area or information without new input
- A shift from engagement to narrowed focus on a single action

These are not failures of performance. The work continues. The tasks are still completed. The change is in how the work is carried, not whether it is done.

2. DECISION POINTS THAT CARRY WEIGHT

Moral injury is often tied to specific types of decisions. These are moments where the available options do not allow for a clean outcome.

Common field examples include:

- Choosing one person, task, or area over another when both require attention
- Ending a search, a shift, or a line of effort while uncertainty remains
- Following protocol when it conflicts with what feels immediately necessary
- Not acting because acting would cause additional harm or exceed capacity

These decisions are often made quickly and without full information. They are also often final, meaning they cannot be revisited in the same conditions.

3. SIGNS IN BEHAVIOR

In the field, moral injury is more often visible in behavior than in words.

You may observe:

- A responder who continues working but avoids certain tasks or areas
- Increased rigidity in following procedures, or the opposite—quiet deviation from them
- Repetition of the same statement or question without resolution
- A change in how a person interacts with others—less eye contact, shorter responses

These changes are usually subtle. They do not stop the work. They exist alongside it.

4. SIGNS IN COMMUNICATION

What is said—and what is not said—can both indicate strain.

You may hear:

- Statements that return to a specific moment or decision
- Questions that cannot be answered but are asked again
- Silence where there would normally be response
- A shift toward purely functional communication with no variation

In some cases, a responder may stop speaking about a particular event entirely, even when others reference it.

5. THE ROLE OF REPETITION

Moral injury often involves repetition.

- Replaying a decision internally
- Rechecking an action that cannot be changed
- Returning to the same question without new information

In the field, this may look like:

- Revisiting the same location after it has been cleared
- Reconfirming the same data point multiple times
- Asking for validation that cannot be provided

Repetition is not inefficiency. It is often an attempt to find resolution where none is available.

6. WHAT IT IS NOT

It is important to distinguish moral injury from other forms of strain.

It is not primarily:

- Fatigue (though fatigue may be present)
- Fear (though risk may be involved)
- Lack of training or competence

A responder experiencing moral injury may still:

- Perform tasks accurately
- Follow procedures

- Maintain outward composure

The difference is not in performance. It is in the weight carried within the performance.

7. WHAT YOU CAN DO IN THE MOMENT

The goal in the field is not to resolve moral injury. It is to support continued functioning without increasing harm.

Helpful responses include:

- Name what is observable
- "You've checked that area twice."
- "You've been on this task a long time."
- Offer a contained action
- "Take five minutes, then we'll decide the next step."
- "Switch tasks with me for a bit."
- Maintain presence without forcing conversation
- Stay nearby
- Work alongside when possible
- Avoid forcing resolution
- Do not try to explain the situation away
- Do not offer reassurances that cannot be confirmed

The aim is not to fix the moment. It is to hold it without adding pressure.

8. AFTER THE MOMENT HAS PASSED

Moral injury does not always surface immediately. It may appear later, when the pace of the work slows or stops.

Indicators after the operation may include:

- Continued focus on a specific decision or outcome
- Difficulty moving past a particular moment in the response

- Avoidance of returning to similar roles or assignments
- A change in how a person relates to the work as a whole

These are not signs that something has gone wrong in the response. They are signs that something remains unresolved.

9. FOR THOSE WHO RECOGNIZE IT IN THEMSELVES

If you recognize these patterns in your own experience:

- You are not alone in this
- The presence of moral weight does not mean you failed
- The lack of a clean answer is part of the condition, not a personal shortcoming

You may not be able to resolve the moment.
But you can:

- Name it
- Acknowledge it
- Carry it with awareness rather than avoidance

10. FINAL NOTE

Moral injury in the field does not always look dramatic. It often appears in small shifts that occur while the work continues.

It is present in:

- the extra second before acting
- the line drawn more heavily than necessary
- the name written where there is no space left

Recognizing it does not remove it.
But it allows you to see what is happening while it is happening.
And that is where responsible care begins.

APPENDIX B

Questions for Reflection and Processing

THESE QUESTIONS ARE NOT meant to be answered all at once. They are not a checklist, and they are not a test. They are offered as a way to return to specific moments from the field and to notice what remains from them.

You may answer them alone, in conversation, or not at all. What matters is not completeness, but honesty in whatever is named.

1. RETURNING TO A SPECIFIC MOMENT

Begin with one moment.

Not the entire operation.

Not the whole story.

One moment that stays with you.

- What happened in that moment?
- Where were you standing?
- Who else was present?
- What was being asked of you at that point?

Stay with what can be described, not what it meant yet.

2. THE DECISION

Focus on what you did.

- What decision did you make?
- What were the available options as you saw them at the time?
- What did you not choose?
- What information did you not have?

Avoid rewriting the moment with what you know now. Stay with what was available then.

3. WHAT COULD NOT BE DONE

Every decision leaves something undone.

- What was left unfinished when you acted?
- Who or what did not receive attention?
- What would have required more time, people, or capacity than was available?

Name what remained, even if it cannot be changed.

4. THE LINE YOU CROSSED (OR DID NOT CROSS)

Some moments involve a boundary.

- Was there a point where you felt a line—something you would or would not do?
- Did you cross it?
- Did you hold it?
- What made that line visible to you?

This may not have been clear at the time. It may be clearer now.

5. WHAT STAYED WITH YOU

After the moment passed:

- What part of it stayed with you?
- Is there an image, a sound, or a specific detail that returns?

- Is there a question that has not settled?

  You do not need to resolve it. Only name it.

6. REPETITION

Notice if the moment repeats.

- Do you find yourself going back to it?
- Do you replay the decision or the outcome?
- Do you check it against what you think should have happened?

Repetition is common. It does not mean you are stuck. It means something has not fully closed.

7. WHAT YOU CARRY FORWARD

Consider what has changed.

- Has this moment affected how you approach similar situations?
- Do you act differently now in certain conditions?
- Has anything become harder to do?
- Has anything become easier?

  Changes may be small. They may also be difficult to name.

8. WHAT YOU WOULD SAY (IF YOU COULD)

There may be something unsaid.

- Is there something you would say to a person involved in that moment?
- Is there something you would say to yourself at that time?
- Is there something you cannot say, even now?

  You do not need to deliver these words. Only recognize them.

9. WHAT OTHERS SAW

Shift perspective slightly.

- How might someone else present have described that moment?
- What would they have seen you do?
- What would they not have known?

This is not to judge the moment, but to widen the frame around it.

10. STAYING WITH IT WITHOUT RESOLVING IT

Some moments do not resolve.

- Can you hold the memory of the moment without forcing an answer?
- Can you acknowledge that more than one thing may be true at the same time?
- Can you let the question remain without closing it too quickly?

Not every moment has a conclusion that fits cleanly.

11. RETURNING TO THE WORK

Finally, consider the present.

- Are you still in this work?
- If so, what allows you to continue?
- If not, what led you to step away?
- What would you need in order to return, if you chose to?

There is no required answer here.

FINAL NOTE

These questions are not meant to produce resolution. They are meant to create space where the reality of the work can be named without being reduced.

You may not arrive at a clear conclusion.

You may not reach an answer that feels complete.

What matters is that the moment is not dismissed or ignored.

It is seen.

And in being seen, it can be carried with greater clarity, even if it cannot be set down.

APPENDIX C

Using These Stories in Training and Care

These stories are not case studies in the traditional sense. They are not meant to be solved, corrected, or improved upon. They present moments where decisions were made under conditions that did not allow for clean outcomes.

This appendix offers ways to use the stories as tools in training, supervision, and care without reducing them to lessons or conclusions.

1. WHAT THESE STORIES ARE FOR

These stories are designed to:

- Surface recognition of moral complexity
- Create space for honest observation
- Support discussion without forcing resolution
- Prepare responders for moments that cannot be fully explained in advance

They are not designed to:

- Teach a "right" decision
- Evaluate performance
- Provide closure

The value is in engagement, not in arriving at answers.

2. SETTING THE ENVIRONMENT

Before using a story, establish the conditions for how it will be received.

- Make clear that there is no single correct interpretation
- Emphasize observation over judgment
- Allow for silence as a valid response
- Set a time boundary so the discussion remains contained

Participants should understand:

- They are not being tested
- They are not required to share personal experiences
- They may step back from discussion if needed

The goal is to create a space that can hold uncertainty without pressure to resolve it.

3. HOW TO INTRODUCE A STORY

When presenting a story:

- Read it aloud or provide it in written form
- Do not summarize or explain it beforehand
- Allow the story to stand on its own

After reading:

- Pause before asking any questions
- Let the room settle
- Do not rush to fill silence

The first response is often not verbal. It may take time before participants are ready to speak.

4. FIRST-LEVEL ENGAGEMENT: WHAT HAPPENED

Begin with observation.

Ask:

- What did you notice?
- What actions took place?
- What changed during the story?

Avoid:

- Why questions at this stage
- Interpretation or evaluation

Keep the focus on what can be seen or described directly.

5. SECOND-LEVEL ENGAGEMENT: THE DECISION

Move to the point of action.

Ask:

- Where was the decision made?
- What options were visible at that moment?
- What was chosen?
- What was not chosen?

Encourage participants to stay within the conditions of the story, not to add information that was not present.

6. THIRD-LEVEL ENGAGEMENT: WHAT REMAINS

Shift to what is left unresolved.

Ask:

- What did not get addressed?
- What remains unclear or incomplete?
- What continues beyond the story?

This stage often reveals the moral weight carried in the moment.

7. FACILITATING WITHOUT FORCING

As a facilitator:

- Do not correct participants' interpretations
- Do not move the group toward agreement
- Do not resolve tension that emerges

If the group becomes quiet:

- Allow the silence
- Do not immediately redirect

If the group becomes overly analytical:

- Return to the story
- Ask what is actually present, not what could be added

Your role is to hold the space, not to direct the outcome.

8. CONNECTING TO FIELD EXPERIENCE (OPTIONAL)

If appropriate, participants may connect the story to their own experience. Offer:

- "Does this remind you of anything you've encountered?"

Do not require:

- Personal disclosure
- Detailed recounting

If someone shares:

- Listen without evaluating
- Do not compare stories
- Do not generalize from a single experience

The connection should remain grounded and voluntary.

9. USE IN TEAM DEBRIEFING

These stories can be used after an operation to support reflection.

- Select a story that parallels the type of decisions encountered

- Read it together as a group
- Use it as a point of entry rather than starting with direct personal questions

This can:

- Reduce pressure on individuals to speak first
- Provide shared language for difficult moments
- Allow reflection without immediate personal exposure

10. USE IN INDIVIDUAL CARE

In one-on-one settings:

- Offer a story as a way to begin conversation
- Ask what stands out to the person reading it
- Allow them to connect—or not connect—it to their own experience

This can:

- Create distance where direct discussion feels too immediate
- Allow reflection without requiring disclosure
- Support gradual engagement with difficult material

11. WHEN TO STOP

Not every discussion needs to reach a conclusion.

End the session when:

- The group has engaged meaningfully
- The time boundary is reached
- The conversation begins to repeat without new insight

Do not extend the discussion in search of closure.
Closure is not the goal.

12. WHAT TO AVOID

When using these stories, avoid:

- Turning them into problem-solving exercises
- Assigning "correct" or "incorrect" decisions
- Using them to evaluate competence
- Forcing emotional responses

These actions reduce the stories to something they are not intended to be.

13. FINAL NOTE

These stories are tools for recognizing what often remains unspoken in the work.

They do not resolve moral tension.

They do not remove uncertainty.

They do not provide answers that apply in every situation.

What they offer is a way to see the moment more clearly while it is happening and after it has passed.

That clarity does not change the conditions of the work.

But it can change how the work is carried.

About the Author

Rev. Gregory C. Smith, PhD, is a Minister of Word and Sacrament in the Presbyterian Church (U.S.A.), now retired after many years of pastoral ministry. His work focuses on moral injury, disaster response, and the lived realities of those who serve in conditions where decisions carry lasting weight.

He has written extensively on faith, public life, and the human cost of responsibility, with multiple books published and forthcoming through Wipf and Stock. His writing brings together theological reflection and field-based insight, shaped by direct engagement with responders, survivors, and care providers.

Rev. Smith serves as a board member of the Iowa Disaster Human Resources Council and remains active in disaster spiritual care. His work continues to support those who seek to remain present, responsible, and human in the midst of crisis.